Hypnosis

EXACT BLUEPRINT on How to Hypnotize Anyone, Including Yourself - Mind Control, Self-Hypnosis, and NLP

Hypnosis

EXACT BLUEPRINT on How to Hypnotize Anyone, Including Yourself - Mind Control, Self-Hypnosis, and NLP

that the author is not engaging in the rendering of legal, financial, medical or professional advice.

Table Of Contents

Bonus   v

Introduction   vii

Chapter 1 – What is Hypnotism   1

Chapter 2 – The Case for Hypnotism   26

Chapter 3 – History of Hypnotism   36

Chapter 4 – Types of Hypnotism   53

Chapter 5 – How to Hypnotize Someone   68

Chapter 6 – Self-Hypnosis   80

Chapter 8 – Guided Imagery   139

Chapter 9 – Benefits of Hypnosis   144

Chapter 10 - Hypnotherapy for Stressed Minds   153

Chapter 11 - Addiction Treatment Process   161

Chapter 12 – Hypnotize with Care   165

Chapter 13: Neuro Linguistic Programming   168

Conclusion   193

Bonus   196

Bonus

Thanks for making it this far in your education. If you want the real multiplier effect and to take your hypnosis skills to the next level, I recommend the easy-to-follow quick tips below to help you unlock more time so you can focus on learning and applying the techniques you care about (e.g. mind control, hypnosis, etc.). No matter what your interests are in life, everyone can benefit from ways to be more productive and time efficient. Minimize time and energy spent on things you don't care about, so you can maximize on what you do!

Visit   https://funnelb.leadpages.co/smarter-not-harder-business/

Top 10 Productivity Tips & Hacks GUARANTEED to Unlock Massive Amounts of Time, Crush Decision Fatigue, and Skyrocket Your Efficiency and Effectiveness

Link: https://funnelb.leadpages.co/smarter-not-harder-business/

Introduction

Welcome and congratulations on choosing this book. Are you frustrated in your life? Is the daily burden of going through routines and schedules taking its heavy toll on your mind? You have come to the right place if you answered yes to both the above questions.

For the longest time, a large portion of society has considered hypnosis a myth. Others have believed in it religiously. Some people have thought of it as dark magic and movies portray it as a scary way to control the minds of others. Because of this, people have developed a negative feeling toward hypnosis. I have written this book in an effort to show the truth behind hypnosis and how it can be helpful in your everyday life.

A person who is hypnotized is completely aware of their surroundings and they are also in control of what is happening to them during the entire process. Hypnosis is a state of semi-consciousness that allows people to access memories that they have blocked out for a variety of reasons. During hypnosis, the person who is hypnotized has a heightened sense of focus and concentration. The person is able to easily concentrate on specific memories, or thoughts, while blocking out all other sources.

Because of the simplicity and access to hypnosis, it is not a surprise that it is used in a wide variety of applications. It allows people to access memories that they would typically never be able to recall without help, which has an extremely valuable basis in a lot of scenarios.

The congratulations mentioned in the above paragraph are for a reason. If you are regularly harangued by stress and strain in your life, you have just found the right key to lock it all away and   never face it. This book has been methodologically designed to help you get rid of daily life stress and attain new levels of self-satisfaction and joy. You will be walked through the various nuances existing between managing your troubles and correcting them. You should not settle for short-term corrections; instead go for long term and more permanent solutions.

Let us delve into what is going to be an informative and fun journey towards your mental emancipation and control. Let us unravel the secrets to implore your mind and find out ways to control it and use it to gain advantage over your life troubles

Chapter 1 – What is Hypnotism

Welcome to the first chapter of this book. We'll talk about X-Men here. Yes, you read that right. If you were familiar with one of Marvel's brilliant creations, you would know about hypnotism.

Hypnotism is the art of influencing minds. You must have heard of the popular name Uri Gagarin, a European who was the first human to display hypnotic powers. He went on to bend a spoon on national television. No, we are not going to read about any magicians. What we are going to read about is very much real and doable, by none other than you. There is also another definition for Hypnotism is an altered state of consciousness where you get direct access to your subconscious mind, which is totally amazing. It is a condition of expanded suggestibility. When a recommendation is acknowledged by the intuitive it is consequently and uncritically followed up on. It is an exceptionally characteristic condition that individuals experience once a day (cases include: parkway entrancing, wandering off in fantasyland, and so forth.

The practice and capability of influencing minds is called hypnotism. It refers to not just the ability to make minds change their direction of thinking but also control which direction this change leads to. In terms of the subject of hypnotism, it signifies a mental state of midway consciousness from where a mind is most likely to react to suggestions and hints. As to what happens after hypnosis, there are generally two theories.

The first theory, the altered theory states that when you are put into a state of hypnosis, you move into a trance state that is nothing but your sleeping consciousness. In other words, everything remains the same except the activity of your consciousness; it is dormant. The second theory argues that when a subject is put under hypnosis, he/she starts acting like how they visualize themselves and not how they really are. The second theory strongly asserts that a state of hypnosis is simply state of role-play action.

To try is to Perfect.

Practice makes a man perfect. Likewise, proper hypnotizing is what it takes to make a perfect hypnotist. But as it said, to write the future neat, it is essential to have read the past thoroughly. So now, we read the past.

To revel in the hypnotic experience, we will have to understand the word from a professional point rather from a dilettante's one, where a person is wheedled into a deep sleep, making the subconscious part of him remains more alert than ever, exterminating the environment's external interferences. To be professional, we never look at flowers. We study the roots. And likewise, we try to understand the concept of hypnosis, as explained by the pioneers.

Dusting the history, we unearth James Braid, a Scottish surgeon as one of the first definers of the Hypnosis, who also happened to coin the term. He first said, that it was a state of nervous sleep, a sleep different from the regular one and defined it as "A peculiar condition of the nervous system, induced by a fixed and abstracted attention of the mental and visual eye, on one subject, not of an exciting nature", and then went on to redefine Hypnotism as state of mental incineration that often leads to enlightened relaxation coined as "nervous sleep". But as time went he admitted and gave in that his original terminology was wrong and misleading. He however revolted that the term "Nervous sleep" should be an alternative for the then existing word monoideism referring to the splinter group of subjects showing symptoms of amnesia.

Michael Nash provides a list of eight definitions of hypnosis by different authors, in addition to his own view that hypnosis is "a special case of psychological regression"

Janet, near the turn of the century, and more recently Ernest Hilgard, has defined hypnosis in terms of dissociation.

Social psychologists Sarbin and Coe have described hypnosis in terms of role theory. Hypnosis is a role that people play; they act "as if" they were hypnotized.

T. X. Barber defined hypnosis in terms of nonhypnotic behavioral parameters, such as task motivation and the act of labeling the situation as hypnosis.

In his early writings, Weitzenhoffer conceptualized hypnosis as a state of enhanced suggestibility. Most recently he has defined hypnotism as "a form of influence by one person exerted on another through the medium or agency of suggestion."

Psychoanalysts Gill and Brenman described hypnosis by using the psychoanalytic concept of "regression in the service of the ego."

Edmonston has assessed hypnosis as being merely a state of relaxation.

Spiegel and Spiegel have implied that hypnosis is a biological capacity.

Erickson is considered the leading exponent of the position that hypnosis is a special, inner-directed, altered state of functioning.

Joe Griffin and Ivan Tyrrell (the originators of the human givens approach) define hypnosis as "any artificial way of accessing the REM state, the same brain state in which dreaming occurs" and they suggest that this definition, when properly understood, resolves "many of the mysteries and controversies surrounding hypnosis". [23]

As time rolled, in 2005 it was from the Society for Psychological Hypnosis, Division 30 of the American Psychological Association the formal definition was provided. "Hypnosis typically involves an introduction to the procedure whereby the subject is informed that suggestions for imaginative experiences will be presented. The hypnotic induction (this is the process of putting a person under hypnosis) is an extended initial suggestion for using an individual's imagination, and may contain further elaborations of the introduction. What is supposed to encourage and push a subject and evaluate responses to suggestions is what is referred to as the 'hypnotic procedure'. When using hypnosis, one person, (referred to as to as the subject) is guided by another, (referred to as the hypnotist) to respond to suggestions for changes in subjective experiences, alterations in perceptions, sensations, emotion, thoughts or behaviors".

It also made the following comments, in the light of hypnosis "Hypnosis typically involves an introduction to the procedure during which the subject is told that suggestions for imaginative experiences will be presented. The hypnotic induction is an extended initial suggestion for using one's imagination, and may contain further elaborations of the introduction. A hypnotic procedure is used to encourage and evaluate responses to suggestions. When using hypnosis, one person (the subject) is guided by another (the hypnotist) to respond to suggestions for changes in subjective experience, alterations in perception, sensation, emotion, thought or behavior. Persons can also learn self-hypnosis, which is the act of administering hypnotic procedures on one's own. If the subject responds to hypnotic suggestions, it is generally inferred that hypnosis has been induced. Many believe that hypnotic responses and experiences are characteristic of a hypnotic state. While some think that it is not necessary to use the word "hypnosis" as part of the hypnotic induction, others view it as essential"

A Venture into technicalities

As the first step of being professional, we brake in through the myths and facts:

Myth: Some people can't be hypnotized.

Fact: Although some researchers and clinicians claim that some people are not able to be hypnotized, everyone has the ability to be hypnotized because it's a natural, normal state that each of us enter at least twice each day – upon awakening and falling asleep. We also enter a hypnotic state whenever we get totally engrossed in a movie or TV show. When the actors become the characters they portray in our minds, we are hypnotized. Also, whenever we are driving and daydreaming enough to miss a turn or freeway exit we know to take, we probably were experiencing a light state of hypnosis.

People may have this misconception because of an unsuccessful experience they've had with a hypnotist. People are responsive to different approaches, and if a particular approach has not been successful in the past, it's a matter of finding the way that works best for them. IMDHA Certified Hypnotherapists/Hypnotists have several techniques that they can use, and are trained to find a method that will work best for you.

Myth: You can be hypnotized to do things against your will

Fact: The hypnosis practitioner is merely a guide or facilitator. He/she cannot "make" you do anything against your will. In fact, during a hypnotic session, you are completely aware of everything going on. In other words, if you do not like where the hypnotist is guiding you, you have the power to reject the suggestions.

This is a commonly held idea that has its source in stage shows and other venues that capitalize on the "power" of the hypnotist. It's worth noting that occasionally a similar issue is raised - "Can someone be hypnotized to do things they wouldn't normally do?" Of course, the answer to that question is "Yes" when you consider that the purpose of hypnosis is often to do things differently than we have done in the past. However, it's notable that these changes are not against the client's will. Hilgard's (1977) work at Stanford demonstrated a principle known as "The Hidden

Observer" which indicates that there is part of the client which monitors the hypnotic process and which will protect them from responding in a manner that violates their ethical and moral standards.

Myth: Under hypnosis you will always tell the truth and could even reveal personal secrets

Fact: You can lie under hypnosis just as easily as in the waking state. In fact, as hypnosis gives you greater access to unconscious resources, you may even be able to tell more creative lies when in trance. Additionally, you are in complete control of what you chose to reveal or conceal.

Myth: I won't remember anything the hypnotist says.

Fact: Everyone experiences hypnosis differently ... for some it's a state in which you are focused on the hypnotists words and listening more carefully, for others it's a little more like day dreaming and your attention may drift and wander from one thought to another ... sometimes not paying any conscious attention to what the hypnotist is saying. Either way is okay, and neither will be more or less effective than the other. It's simply a matter of your own personal style.

Myth: A person can get stuck in a trance forever.

Fact: No one has ever been stuck in a hypnotic trance. Hypnosis is a naturally occurring state that we enter and exit during the normal course of a day. There are no known or reported dangers with hypnosis when working with a trained practitioner. If the hypnotist fails to emerge someone from hypnosis, he/she will return to a fully alert state on their own. Depending on that person's need for sleep, he/she will either drift on into a natural sleep or simply emerge to full consciousness spontaneously within minutes.

When in the state of hypnosis, our brainwaves vacillate through the Alpha to Theta ranges. Any time you choose to emerge from hypnosis, for any reason, you are able to simply open your eyes and become fully alert. If you were practicing self-hypnosis before going to bed and ended in the Delta state, then it would mean you'd simply fall asleep.

Myth: Intelligent people can't be hypnotized

Fact: Quite the contrary, studies suggest that people of above average intelligence who are capable of concentrating and who have a capacity for creativity and vivid imagination usually make the best subjects.

Myth: A person under hypnosis is asleep or unconscious.

Fact: Hypnosis is neither sleep nor unconsciousness, even though a common misconception is that you are asleep when hypnotized. The experience of a formally induced hypnotic state might resemble sleep from the physical point of view: slowed breathing, eyes closed, muscles relaxed, activity decreased. From the mental standpoint the client is generally relaxed and may be keenly alert, in a comfortable state where the person can think, talk and even move about if needed. But all clients are unique and can experience hypnosis in their own unique ways. Some are comfortable enough with the process that they find themselves drifting in and out of a more dream-like state. In some instances they might respond unconsciously, through ideomotor signals or other methods. Less often employed, there are certain few uses in which, under the direction of a specially trained hypnotherapist, the client can generate unconsciousness for the purposes of surgical anesthesia or the management of acute pain, or in certain emergency situations that might warrant it.

Myth: Hypnosis is contrary to religious beliefs

Fact: Hypnosis can be used to ease or remove pain, overcome fears, phobias, addiction and other problems. While a handful of religious sects have raised objections to hypnosis, today most religious groups accept the proper ethical use of hypnosis for helping people. Included are Roman Catholic, Orthodox, and most Protestant Christian Churches as well as Judaism, Hinduism, Buddhism and others. Hypnosis is not associated with any of the world religions. A professional and ethical hypnotist respects the faith of clients and will not use it inappropriately to influence a person's religious beliefs.

The next step of being professional, rather a layman, is understanding the concept of hypnotism, for which we will have to start with understanding the technical terms and the explanation of the above said definitions.

Suggestion:
A man with no light shed, or to shed, would believe that the suggestions are the words spoken by the hypnotist to get the person relaxed and focused. But as hypnotists, we must know better. And the better, is this. As in every field, the field of hypnotism also has its own conflict of ideologies. The way the word 'suggestion' is comprehended by the hypnotist is one such confliction. One ideological stream of hypnotist believe that suggestion is a medium of communication between the hypnotist and the conscious

9

state of mind while the on the other side of the balance, there are hypnotists who emphasis that the term refers to the appeal made by the hypnotist to the subconscious, or otherwise coined, the unconscious part if mind. Sigmund Freud and Pierre Janet brought these concepts into light, in the 19th century. Sigmund Freud came up with the theory called the Psychoanalytic Theory that explains the fact that the conscious line of thoughts is lined up in the surface of the thoughts and those unconscious line are hidden deep down the surface of the mind.

Subject:

Subject is the person who is being hypnotized by the hypnotist. They are people who have sought hypnosis as a cure, to work through some issues, to overcome their deepest phobias, or anxieties that has haunted them. It might not only be that way, but to be broad, even physical ailments can be attended to with the help of hypnosis.

Hypnotist:

Here we go. This is us! But not just us! Not yet. This is us, after ardent practices and depth understandings about the methods of hypnosis. So, generally, a hypnotist is a person who after years of practical and theoretical training is ready enough to take the subject through the process of hypnosis to get the results that the subject desires to attain.

We must, come to the understanding that, the subject and the hypnotist needn't always be two different individuals. In other words, there is no necessity that a person to another should perform hypnosis. The hypnotist can as well be the subject, in which case, the same is called self-hypnosis. Self- hypnosis means administering the hypnotic procedures to one self. Self-hypnotism is a tool for self-control and can be used to regulate your mental deviations, desires, urges and cravings. Besides the ones mentioned, it can further be used to gain control over your overall mental state. Let us start our journey without further ado.

Conscious and subconscious minds

As we learn that hypnosis all about the subconscious part of the subject, we might as well clarify what exactly is subconscious mind. Think of the subconscious mind as the storage room of everything that is currently not in your conscious mind.

The Conscious Mind (10-12 %): Normally, you are only aware of the thought processes in your conscious mind. You consciously think over the problems that are right in front of you, consciously choose words as you speak, consciously try to remember where you left your keys. But in doing all these things, your conscious mind is working hand-in-hand with your subconscious mind

It is like the CPU of a computer with current rules of life

Its functions include thinking, finding logic, feeling, and analyzing, deciding, controlling voluntary body movements

The conscious mind exercises what we call will power.

It is also the place of working memory (memory we use every day to function).

Sub conscious mind:

The subconscious mind stores all of your previous life experiences, your beliefs, your memories, you skills, all situations you've been through and all images you've ever seen.

The best way to understand the subconscious mind is to look at the example of the person who wants to learn how to drive a car. At the beginning he wouldn't be able to hold a conversation with anyone while driving, as he would be focusing on the different moves involved. That's because he's still using his conscious mind to drive.

The subconscious mind; your Autopilot!

Few weeks later driving becomes a natural habit that happens automatically without needing to think about it. That person could even start using his cell phone or talking to his friends while driving.

This happened because the driving habit has been transferred to his subconscious mind and so the conscious mind become free. This allowed him to use it to talk in his cell phone.

The subconscious mind is responsible for the automatically triggered feelings and emotions that you suddenly experience upon facing a new situation. If you were about to give a presentation then all the fear and anxiety feelings you might experience are in fact launched and controlled by your subconscious mind.

The conscious mind is, on the other hand, responsible for logic, calculations and all actions that are performed while you are conscious. The subconscious mind also controls other functions in your body like breathing and heartbeats.

Another good example that can help you better understand the subconscious mind is the process of breathing. Before you started reading the previous line your breathing was controlled by your subconscious.

I want you now to try and control your breathing for one minute. You will be able to do so of course. This time it was the conscious mind that was controlling your breathing, but when you let go of your focus your subconscious mind will take over again.

Program your subconscious mind

When the information about driving is stored into your subconscious mind it's stored as a program. Think of your mind as a computer and the driving information as software that can be run automatically whenever needed.

The same goes for lots of other activities and emotions. If someone annoyed you the installed program of anger is going to be launched and the result will be a behavior that you may regret later.

By programming the subconscious mind with new programs you can fix many problems in your personality. Just make sure that your autopilot is capable of running your system without ruining your life or causing you any problems.

Programming your subconscious can be done through hypnosis. The subconscious mind learns by repetition and not by logic. This is why you can convince someone to believe in something by repeating your argument again and again rather than using logic. For more information on this topic see the guide to the psychology of convincing

Rules of the subconscious mind

In order to best use the power of your subconscious mind you must first know how the subconscious mind works. The subconscious mind is governed by many rules.

Learning about these rules will allow you to make the best use out of your subconscious mind with the least effort. At the bottom of the article is a link that contains all the information you need to know about the rules of the subconscious mind.

Ego defense mechanisms

Just like your body has got its defenses against physical wounds and injuries your subconscious mind has got its defenses against emotional shocks and wounds.

These are called ego defense mechanisms or unconscious defense mechanisms. The ego defense mechanisms' main function is to protect your well being and to help you overcome emotional shocks.

The subconscious mind and forgetting about someone

The main reason people stay broken after breakups is that they have false beliefs about relationships stored in their subconscious minds. In my book, how to get over anyone in few days, I described how getting rid of can beliefs like "the one" or "the soul mate" help you forget about anybody in few days.

As soon as someone gets rid of these beliefs he will realize that he can one day find another person who replaces the one who left him and so recovery happens.

Using your conscious and subconscious mind together

The conscious and the subconscious mind can make a great team if you used them together. The first can handle some tasks then assigns them to the second while the second can send feedback and messages about the task in the form of emotions to the first.

Emotions are no more than messages sent by your subconscious mind in order to notify you about something. By learning how to make the best use of the cooperation between your conscious and subconscious mind your life skills will improve and you will have much more control over your emotions.

How does hypnosis work on subconscious mind?

Hypnosis works by updating the unconscious / subconscious mind with new and more helpful information, like reprogramming a computer.

Hypnosis is a much easier way to bypass the critical filter. Under hypnosis, the critical filter goes to sleep for a while. The Conscious Mind stays awake, and can still make decisions. But now you're in control while your subconscious is receptive to any suggestion that your conscious mind wants to let in.

Induction:

A state where the subject, (The person who is being hypnotized), responds to the suggestions, communication used by the hypnotist (The one who hypnotizes) is called the Hypnotic Induction. Further, we will learn what is Induction and the methods of it.

Why induce? The hypnotist, to unearth, or to dust the long forgotten memories, takes the subjects into a hypnotic trance state. The induction can either be to just open up the blocks and to freshen up the memories or to find a particular piece of information blurred out into the abyss. It might also be to do absolutely nothing, nothing but to let go.

How to induce?

The next big question. There are quite a few methods by which the hypnotist can induce the subject. The prerequisites and dos and don'ts you will have to know before learning the methods of hypnosis is,

1. Find a subject

Choose a subject who must be willing to become the guinea pig of your hypnosis experiment. This person must be told everything you are going to do to him in detail. Getting free consent of your subject is of prime importance for ethical reasons. Make sure you introduce to them all the things you will be saying and gain their confidence. Hypnotizing someone is more about gaining trust than making someone fall asleep. If the subject is confident that they are in safe hands, half your work is done then and there.

2. Inquire about Previous Experiences

Have a casual talk with your subject about their previous experiences or run-ins with hypnotism anywhere or any time in their life. Ask them about their experience and how they responded to it. This knowledge can help you measure the kind of subject you are dealing with.

3. Reassurance

It is very important that your subject is able to trust you as his guide. Reassure your subject that they are going to remember each and every detail so asked or uttered in the conversation post hypnosis. Let me tell you a secret here; this is a big lie. They are not going to remember everything they said but you're telling them so builds confidence.

4. Place

Choose a quaint place to perform the hypnosis. This place should be well lighted and quiet. Make sure no sort of disturbance is able to penetrate the place for the time you will be performing your work.

5. Induce a thought

Start off by asking the subject to close their eyes and enter a happy place of their own creation. Again, imagination comes into play as it all depends on how well the subject is able to think. You could make your own suggestions like a green lush meadow with a crystal clear stream running by.

6. Fill in the details

Now that you have induced a thought in your subject's mind and helped them walk towards what they think is their happy place, it's time to fill their mind with tiny yet intricate details. Ask them what they see around them when they are walking in their happy place. Ask them the color of their shoes, or the shape of their top. These details are not present but as you keep asking, the subject keeps creating. You are hence, not really asking, but helping create.

7. Instruct

Start modifying your tone from suggestive to instructive. Use words like 'Do it', instead of "could you try it?" Slowly but surely the subject will fall into your manipulation trap and start repeating what you say or responding to what you ask. Do not cross the ethical boundary of not asking anything they would not like to answer in otherwise normal conditions.

8. Provide Positivity

While the subject is still in the state of hypnosis, utter statements that are positive and energetic in nature. If the goal of your session is for the subject to get rid of a bad habit, talk to them in instructive tones and with positive sentences like:
"You deserve better than falling prey to this bad habit"
"I have faith in you; you can overcome this"
"There is nothing that you cannot do."
"Do not give up; fight it and it will go away."

9. A Slow End

The best way to end such a hypnosis session is to first say it loudly that you are going to count till five, at the end of which they will gradually wake up from their sleep. In a firm tone, count from one to five with at least two seconds of gap between two consecutive numbers.

10. Relax

Do not engage the subject in sudden and exhausting activities immediately after they have woken up. Give them some time to spend alone and ask them to not think too much on what just happened. Tell them that they'd brilliantly and are now rid of whatever trouble they had.

Depth Levels of Hypnosis:

Some subjects will encounter more profound levels of hypnosis than others. The more profound the level, the higher the level of impact your proposals will apply. As a stage subliminal specialist, it is imperative to comprehend the different profundity levels of Hypnosis and the related phenomena of each. There are four essential stages of Hypnosis:
1) Hypnotical;
 2) Light Trance;
3) Medium Trance; and
4) Deep Trance—also called "Sleepwalking," a state in which an individual performs activities suitable to the waking state while really profound sleeping. Individuals

who walk or talk in their rest are displaying somnambulistic conduct behavior.

Key Factor of Deep Hypnosis:

While the reality of the matter is that all individuals can be hypnotized to some degree on the other hand, it is evaluated just around 20% are potential somnambulists, too alluded to as "hypnotics"–people who have the ability to enter deep hypnosis. This little, yet very suggestible sections of the populous make the best subjects for entrancing stage exhibition. This is not to say that all subjects who are not somnambulists ought to be barred from you're training. In fact, a remarkable opposite is valid. By figuring out how to effectively hypnotize even subjects with lesser sleep inducing abilities, you will have gotten to be much more proficient at taking care of exceptionally suggestible subjects in front of an audience. In addition to regular capacity, there are two different variables that influence a subject's capacity to enter a profound condition of hypnosis–cooperation or resistance (either cognizant or oblivious) and inspiration. This recent variable is as a rule increased in an inwardly charged circumstance, for example, a live performance. The splendid lights, music, riddle, crowd, and desires of uncommon occasions in a stage demonstrate all assistance to increase this impact.

One last note, a subject's normal ability to enter profound hypnosis can develop altogether with each effective hypnosis session. This procedure shapes the premise of the "rehypnotization" system. It is an imposing device for rapidly extending hypnosis in exceedingly suggestible subjects and further screening out the individuals who are definitely not.

Rehypnozization

We realize that rehashed hypnotization's make it less demanding for a subject to enter Hypnosis. It is similar to a competitor preparing the body to perform in a certain way, but the hypnotic subject is molding his or her psyche. Each time a subject experiences hypnosis and stirs, that individual's capacity to focus more eagerly and concentrate on the administrator's recommendations makes improvements.

This idea frames the premise of the hypnotization procedure that means that you speak the truth to learn. It is a to a great degree successful instrument for developing the level of hypnosis in exceptionally powerless subjects— especially after a fast (mass) incitement in front of an audience. In addition to this, it gives you a priceless instrument for further screening out those without the ability to enter deep hypnosis.

Here's the means by which it reaches up to your expectations. The gathering of subjects considering stage is informed that in a minute you will wake them each one in turn. When they open their eyes, these straightforward strategies will offer assistance guarantee you accomplish the most profound conceivable levels of hypnosis in your subjects and as an outcome, the most noteworthy level of vulnerability to your proposals. Close their eyes and investigate yours, they will fall once again into a significantly deeper, more solid sleep than some time recently. The administrator approaches every subject and summons the individual to investigate his eyes as he recommends, "Your eyes are getting heavier, very heavy. You can't keep them open any more, close your eyes also, go to sleep. On the off chance that any subject neglects to react and re-enter hypnosis, that individual is instantly rejected. Next, the staying responsive subjects are awakened as a gathering and again told when they investigate the hypnosis specialist's eyes; they will fall once more into a significantly deeper sleep. Once more, lethargic subjects are rejected. The subjects might now be given a gathering test with the included (compound) recommendation that its consummation will send them down significantly. You get the thought. This strategy works—so use it.

More Strategies

In addition to the best possible timing, reiteration and conveyance of proposals, here are some different ways you can pick up an edge in affecting subjects:

1. Manufacture early victories. Since the effect of your recommendations develops with every achievement and lessens with every disappointment, dependably start with tests that offer you the most noteworthy probability of achievement and advancement to progressively all the more difficult ones.

2. Get subjects into an early pattern of compliance. Voluntary responses to instructions increase acceptance to involuntary suggestions later. In other words, when you tell a subject to sit or stand, hold out his arm in a certain way, etc., the uncritical way in which the subject complies will often carry over to hypnotic suggestions as well.

3. Use checking to escalate the impact of a recommendation. At whatever point suitable, recommend that on the tally of three, five, and so forth. The subject will do such also, such. This intense system helps sign the subject as to the accurate minute in time a craved reaction is normal.

4. Utilize non-verbal proposals to fortify verbal ones. Dramatic artistry is a natural segment of stage hypnosis. Non-verbal recommendations as physical signals, body developments, and in addition to that breathing, can all help impact the result.

5. Exploit the force of mass proposal. Recommendations to a gathering, for example, a board of trustees, are constantly more successful than those to an individual subject. Subjects in a gathering have a tendency to lose their hindrances and are additionally impacted by the effective reactions of different subjects.

Working with Individual Subjects:

The primary step on your way to mastering hypnotism influence, is figuring out how to actuate hypnosis in individual subjects. This is a standout amongst the most critical aptitudes you will get and its dominance is basic to your further improvement as a hypnosis specialist. The most successful impelling of hypnosis dependably starts with assent. The subject may make this acknowledgment deliberately or unknowingly. In either case, the net result is the same; the subject "expects" to be hypnotized. It must be comprehended that there are incalculable hypnosis strategies in presence. There is nobody right or wrong strategy. All are similarly great, insofar as they offer certainty to the administrator and confidence to the subject, as examined in Chapter One. The main motivation behind any system for hypnosis is to think the subject's consideration and in this way to take out the majority of the exasperating impacts while leaving yet a solitary channel of recommendation, which is normally the voice of the hypnosis specialist and the ear of the subject.

So-called passes—the use of the hands and arms to direct vitality toward the subject amid the induction—are totally superfluous. These are really a leftover from the nineteenth century. Indeed, even in this way, numerous cutting edge stage hypnosis inducers still utilize such emotional signals as a type of acting skill. This is fine; in as much as it is comprehended there is no experimental premise for their utilization. Nor, arrives any need to touch a subject's brow, hand, knee, etc.—in general, no substantial contact is needed. One's voice is an adequate channel of correspondence.

Practice the accompanying hypnotic affectation procedure, one-on-one, with a wide scope of subjects until you have the capacity to effectively impact the larger part of them. Every single outside diversion ought to be wiped out or minimized as much as conceivable. At the outset, be arranged to hold up to ten minutes or more for a subject to achieve a condition of hypnosis. Try not to stress, rate will accompany time. The most imperative thought when beginning is taking in the best possible system.

EXACT BLUEPRINT on How to Hypnotize Anyone, Including Yourself - Mind Control, Self-Hypnosis, and NLP

One of the key parts of most hypnotic incitement procedures is the centering of the subject's consideration on an "object of obsession." This item is held or suspended in position around one foot before the subject. It ought to additionally be just sufficiently high (over the subject's head), so it causes the individual to raise his or her eyes somewhat upward to think consideration. Such position is favorable to exhausting the eyes that, unexpectedly, possess pretty nearly the same position as ordinary sleep.

If you are wondering about the things you might need to get the subject focused on, this can be a coin, gem, emblem, ball, or a pocket watch dangling from a chain—as frequently connected with sleep inducing actuation in the well-known media. Objects that reflect light back toward the subject are best suited to this task.

Chapter 2 – The Case for Hypnotism

Seldom does hypnosis work in the way the media in general and pop culture in particular portrays it. No, it isn't a devious taskmaster who waves a pocket watch or whose eyes swirl like mad right in front of you to make you gullible, err I mean suggestible. It also isn't about how Rosario Dawson's character in the movie Trance turns James McAvoy's character into Thomas Crown, how the bedazzling looks of the famous Hypno Toad is glorified nor is it about those the glorious promises of riches, happiness and sexy bodies by Paul McKenna.

To date, continuous discussions, debates or even arguments rage concerning whether or not hypnosis actually has any viable uses aside from making an otherwise sane person bark like a dog at the snap of a hypnotist's fingers – assuming that's even possible of course. Then there's the discussions about self-hypnosis. One thing's for sure that everybody can agree on is this – hypnosis isn't for everyone. It can even be challenging to prove that it does work for some because its results or authenticity can't be measured objectively, i.e., with numbers and statistical analysis. At least with things like medicines or manufacturing processes, you can measure the results with numbers and run statistical analyses on them. With hypnosis, all that can be banked on are the words of the people who were hypnotized.

As such, the question becomes even more important: does hypnosis really work or is it even real? Is it safe to say that the United States Military made the mistake of spending countless number of hours – and dollars – in using hypnosis to brainwash the population or that hypnosis is real because the military did use it? Or can we say with certainty that celebrity hypnotists like Keith Barry and Paul McKenna are just plain hucksters?

That I believe in hypnosis is quite obvious by my writing this book. Allow me to make the case for hypnosis with the following pieces of evidence that I find to be compelling enough to at least warrant your further investigation on the topic.

Hypnosis and Kicking The (Smoking) Habit

It seems like celebrity hypnotists like Paul McKenna aren't as hucksters as many anti-hypnosis people portray them to be. McKenna has made a fortune selling his self-help products that include books, audio recordings, videos and seminars. In all of these, he gives the promise of successfully making money, losing excess weight and giving up smoking.

Well at least, he's spot on when it comes to kicking the smoking habit. How can I say that? Well, there have been many published empirical studies that found hypnosis to be highly effective in terms of helping people ditch the cigs. Just how effective?

Consider that on average, hypnosis was found to exhibit a 90.6% chance for successfully kicking the habit within 6 months to 3 years and that about 87% of people who underwent hypnotherapy for quitting reportedly continued to abstain from the nicotine buffet after more than 3 years.

That being said, why are nicotine patches still selling like hotcakes, huh?

Hypnosis Has Been Used as A Substitute for Drugs

While it's been established that hypnosis can help satiate cravings for low-level drugs such as cigarettes, can it do just as well with more potent stuff like coke, meth, alcohol and other illegal drugs? Well, studies have also shown that hypnosis can greatly increase one's chances of weaning themselves off addiction to such potent substances and staying clean. A study done during – when else? – the 1960s tried to see if the mind-altering "benefits" of LSD can be duplicated without the stuff. The result? Yes, it can be done. The study was able to do so simply by asking the subjects to think about what happened and how they felt during the last time they did LSD.

So why would people shoot such stuff up their system if the only reason for doing so, i.e., the "high", can be easily enjoyed with hypnosis? It only makes so much sense because hypnosis is about tapping the unconscious mind, which is what hallucinogenic drugs like LSD actually do.

Many creative geniuses have been known to use drugs to "unleash" their creativity by tapping the unconscious mind. But consider the surrealist writer Andre Breton. He used hypnosis from time to time to spur himself to write automatically.

Cure for The Head and Missing Limbs

Alright – maybe the word "cure" isn't the appropriate word to use. Still, hypnosis – being all about tapping into the unconscious mind – is a good way to manage mental issues or problems. Several studies have shown that hypnosis – leading a person into a state of trance and suggesting to them that they're no longer or are less depressed or anxious – has beneficial effects in terms of managing such mental or emotional concerns. Hypnosis has been used to reduce or minimize anxiety concerning surgeries – both prior and post – particularly in people who don't want to undergo it out of fear or wrong beliefs.

Hypnosis is also proven by studies to be an effective method for dealing with what's called the Phantom Limb Syndrome, which is when people who've lost a limb still feel as if it's still there. The problem lies when they feel "intense pain" in limbs that are no longer there. Hypnosis can help people reduce, minimize or even cure Phantom Limb Syndrome.

It's All About the Glaze

No, I'm not talking about donuts, chicken or other delicious food items. I'm talking about the eyes of hypnosis subjects. And again, I'm not talking about coating them with caramel.

Ok, now I have that out of the way, let's get back to hypnosis and glaze, shall we? You see, one of the most compelling arguments against hypnosis, particularly stage hypnosis, is that it needs all parties involved to be in on it for it to work. In simpler terms, it's believed that the supposed hypnosis subject needs to "fake" it. But science is here to the rescue!

Scientists from 3 leading European schools – University of Skovde (Sweden), University of Turku (Sweden) and Aalto University (Finland) – studied extensively the effect of hypnosis on subjects' eyes. Mainly, they studied a woman who's able to enter a deep state of hypnotic trance very quickly, seemingly in an instant by just saying a key word.

As she entered a hypnotic trance, they utilized several high tech gadgets to observe any changes in her eyes prior to and right after the hypnotic trance. And they found that under a real hypnotic trance, the eyes of the subject were glazed. Now I don't know about you but glazed eyes are quite challenging to recreate – unless you're a zombie or something.

The fact that hypnosis subjects' eyes become glazed is another compelling piece of evidence for the case for hypnosis.

Memory Boost

For many self-help gurus, one of the most popular – and often under delivered or abused – promises are significant improvement in memory. They go as far as promising they can help you become a better public speaker, ensure that you'll never misplace your car keys and and prevent countless other things that are affected by poor memory.

While the popular or en vogue way of improving memory these days is via mental organization of memories, e.g., mental filing or storage cabinets, hypnosis provides a much simpler – and easier – way to improve memory. Even if there's much discussion on whether or not it actually helps you remember things much better, there are researches that do suggest it can. Because both hypnosis and better memory is all about accessing that part of the mind that's normally hard or almost impossible to access on a conscious level, hypnosis makes perfect sense when it comes to improving memory.

Sleight of Mouth Exists

It's common knowledge that the underlying principle for practically all the tricks that magicians use is the sleight of hand, which is all about using hand movements to conceal or reveal what needs to be in order to successfully create the illusion of magic. While magic doesn't exist, sleight of hand is real. It's what makes magic look real.

While hypnosis isn't like magic in the sense that magic tricks are merely just tricks, they both rely on sleight techniques. The difference being is that magic tricks rely on sleight of hand while hypnosis uses sleight of mouth. It's part of a thing that's called covert hypnosis, which is the exact total opposite of the type of hypnosis done on stage. The thing with covert hypnosis is that unlike complicit or stage hypnosis that makes subjects aware that they're being hypnotized, covert hypnosis involves subjects being suggested to without them noticing it. Scary!

Nah, it isn't. It's basically similar to using subliminal images on hypnosis subjects – like what practically all commercials and ads are trying to do to us unsuspecting consumers – whereby some operant or trigger words or phrases are continuously uttered to the subject when they're in a completely suggestible state of mind. Covert hypnosis subconsciously suggests to the minds of subjects without being noticed. It's pretty much similar to what Leo's and Joseph's characters do in the movie Inception except that covert hypnosis does this while the subject's awake.

Famous People Use It

I know it may sound rather superficial and shallow an argument for hypnosis but if famous people use it and they're successful, it means hypnosis is real and it works. Consider one of the best golfers in the world since time immemorial – Tiger Woods. He used hypnosis as a way of blocking out practically all distractions to be able to focus intensely on the game. Well, practically everything except mistresses. But still, you can't argue with his great golfing success and hypnosis helped him a lot.

Albert Einstein was also known to have used hypnosis, particularly self-hypnosis, and legend has it that it was in one of his trances that he was able to formulate the theory of relativity. Now if that's not a cool benefit of hypnosis, I don't know what is!

The Government Uses It

The U.S. Government, particularly through the CIA, has done and continues to do many covert and seemingly secret stuff like the MKUltra mind control program. Said program grew out of the government's hypnosis experiments and in this program, American war veterans and young men alike were allegedly tortured and drugged for the sake of studying mind control. While the program itself has mutated from its humble beginnings, its roots can be traced to hypnosis, which means that the government acknowledges its substance. In some documents that were declassified several years ago, the viability of hypnosis in interrogating subjects was set out by the CIA. Said studies suggest that hypnosis success was much higher in people who were already sleeping, who were doing their best to avoid getting into a hypnotic trance and when their personalities were already suggestible.

Long History of Being Studied

A big chunk of the CIA's portfolio of evidences favoring hypnosis can be traced to extensive and numerous studies on the subject that were conducted since time immemorial. Consider this – if hypnosis isn't real, then why would records on studies on the subject matter continue to persist from as far back as even the 18th century? If there's smoke, and a long standing one at that, there must be an actual fire!

All throughout world history, practically every civilization and culture has had accounts of its people getting into states and trances that can easily be identified as hypnotic. China and India – two of the oldest and most established civilizations on Earth – have ancient documents telling how surgical pains were relieved using hypnotism even while the idea of real anesthetics was still centuries away from being conceptualized.

Emanating from there, hypnosis as a supplement to surgical practices was imported in Europe when in 1974, Jacob Grimm (of Grimm's Fairy Tales) emerged safely from a tumor-removing surgery using only hypnosis (through story-telling) as an anesthetic. Hypnosis was also used to treat post-traumatic stress disorders in war veterans.

The Placebo Reality

If there's one thing that brings the placebo effect and hypnosis together, it is the fact that both are dependent on the powers of belief and suggestions. As such, it's practically impossible to create placebo control that's credible when it comes to hypnotism. That being said, the placebo effect and hypnotism may very well be of the same essence.

Even if the reason for the placebo effect continues to remain a mystery, science has validated its existence. Numerous pharmaceutical studies were already – and continue to be – conducted where subjects took pills or "medicines" that contained no real and active ingredients (placebos) and were simply told how those "medicines" will help alleviate their conditions. In many cases, placebos performed as well as the actual medicines (placebo effect). And in some rare cases, the placebos actually outperformed the real medicines. Considering that placebos have no real active ingredients, it can only mean that what made the difference is what the subjects believed the placebos will do, which was influenced by the suggestions made by the researchers. It then becomes about "deceiving" the mind into believing something, e.g., that placebos are effective. Hypnotism anyone?

Chapter 3 – History of Hypnotism

Hypnotism has been around since ancient times and in fact the entire concept and development of hypnotherapy and hypnosis can be found in ancient documents and texts. Hypnosis was in practice for several centuries but gained massive popularity only in the 18th century. It is believed that the French were the first to develop and fine tune hypnosis and make it into a practicing art form. In the 1840s James Braid was the one who coined the term hypnotism. In this technique he believed that hypnosis was more of self centered approach and awareness rather than just mesmerizing somebody. There are several texts and documents that throw significance of hypnosis. While many believed that the French were the original founders, there are several scripts from forgotten eras, which prove otherwise.

According to several historians like Will Durant, he didn't believe that the French founded hypnotism. He believed that the Indians used hypnotism as a tool. He believed that the Hindus found in India were the first to practice hypnotism extensively. Gurus, Rishis and other hermits practiced the art of meditation, concentration and focus. This was believed to be done to communicate with the Hindu gods and goddesses. Also people who fell sick in ancient India were taken to monks who sat and meditated at temples. These monks cured the problems and ailments of the people who came to them through hypnosis. Other sources claim that Avicenna from Persia distinguished between hypnotic trance and sleep. This Persian psychologist stated the differences in his book 'The Book of Healing'. In this book he states that hypnosis is a state in which a person can induce conditions and situations to one person and the other person can accept this as reality.

There has also been wide speculation about magnetism and mesmerism in hypnotism. It is also believed that hypnotism was developed through these two. For instance, Valentine Greatrakes from Ireland became popular due to his ability to use magnets and heal his patients. He was termed as "the Great Irish Stroker" due to his talent. Paracelsus was a physician from Switzerland who used magnets to heal people, which were proved to be very effective. A Catholic priest called Johann Joseph Gassner healed people through hypnotism. He advocated that those diseases that were caused by evil spirits would leave the body through meditation and prayer. In the 17th century, Father Maximilian Hell who was a Jesuit from Vienna used magnets by placing them on the body of the patients to heal them. One of his apprentices was Franz Anton Mesmer, who developed modern forms of hypnosis.

Franz Anton Mesmer was an Austrian physicist, who revolutionized hypnosis. He researched and developed something known as mesmerism, which is alternatively known as animal magnetism. In this form he distinguished between traditional magnetism that was done with the use of magnets and animal magnetism that referred to the force that each person possessed inside them. Human beings and animals could exercise this force in order to enhance themselves. Inspirited by the works of Richard Mead who was an English physician, Franz Anton Mesmer discovered that after a patient bled they were able to develop a resistance by using a magnet and passing it over the cut. The magnetic force made the bleeding stop. He gained massive popularity in France especially with the rich and influential citizens of France for his ability to cure people using magnets. It was at this point that the medical community faced stiff competition from him and hence put forth a challenge. Heeding to the request of the medical community, the French aristocrats and kings formulated a board consisting of a chemist called Lavoisier, a medical doctor whose expertise lied in controlling pain called Joseph Ignace Guillotin and Benjamin Franklin. Mesmer refused to participate in this challenge and refused to answer any questions that the board put forward. He instead made his apprentice Dr. D'Eslon who experimented on a patient. He blindfolded the patient and the results showed the responsiveness of the patient in comparison to that of a tree, which has been magnetized. The board accepted this and believed that mesmerism could be put into practice only by using the imagination. Though, this form of therapy is an alternate form that has gained massive popularity, Mesmer kept to himself and retired to Switzerland where he subsequently died.

With Mesmer's coinage came a lot of support. There were several advocated of this style of practice. During the French revolution, mesmerism was used to control the crowd. In fact, ancient texts and records give detailed description on how the French aristocrats brought together people who practiced this art. There are suggestions made stating that social order could be restored through mesmerism. It was at that period that magnetism started to wear off. People stopped using magnetism extensively and switched to mesmerism. Abbé

Faria was an Indo Portuguese priest who channeled the interest of the public into animal magnetism. He formulated what the Parisians knew as oriental hypnosis in the 19th century. He hailed from India and traveled across the world and exhibited his style of magnetism. He did not make use of patients nor did he confirm to medical reasons. He also did not manipulate to achieve results. The major difference between the mesmerism style developed by Mesmer and Faria's oriental hypnosis was that Faria believed that the forces were developed from the mind of the person. Through cooperation and training, people could project themselves a lot better and enhance their minds. His style of hypnosis was researched upon, extended and case studied by practitioners like Hippolyte Bernheim and Ambroise-Auguste Liébeault. The framework that Faria had developed and the extension and fine tuning of Faria's theories by several people contributed to the development of new techniques like the autogenic training techniques which was developed by Johannes Heinrich Schultz and the autosuggestion techniques which were founded by Émile Coué. Marquis de Puységur was the first to introduce the term somnambulism. He was an apprentice of Mesmer and his followers and disciples were called Experimentalists. They were advocated of the theory of Paracelsus Mesmer fluidism.

Like stated before the exact founding of hypnotism is unknown and there are several texts from the 18th century. One of these is those of Récamier who used a certain form of hypnotism before its actual founding and popularity. He was a physician who used a type of hypnotism that was similar to hypnoanesthesia where he cured his patients after lulling them into a mesmeric coma. After him, Carl Reichenbach researched extensively on this energy that Récamier used. Though several believed that Récamier possessed magical and supernatural powers, Carl Reichenbach tried to find a scientific explanation to this energy. This energy was termed after the Norse god Odin and was called Odic force. The scientific community that existed rejected all of Reichenbach's arguments and explanations. It was in 1846, after the publishing of the literary work called 'The Power of the Mind over the Body' by James Braid that Reichenbach's explanation was termed as pseudoscientific.

However, extensive use of hypnotism in some form or the other spread. This was exclusive to the 18th century alone. In fact, the mesmeric sleep technique was used as an anesthetic in British occupied India. Physician James Esdaile operated upon about 350 people by lulling them into a state of conscious coma through mesmeric practices. This was used before the advent of chemical anesthetic. This practice was significantly reduced after chemical anesthetic was discovered. Hypnosis was still used in certain inaccessible pockets of the world. A surgeon called John Elliotson from England also carried this out. He used hypnosis to perform operations. These operations proved to be successful and painless due to the use of hypnosis.

James Braid served as a surgeon and was from Scotland. He was the first to coin the term hypnotism. He advocated this in his book Practical Essay on the Curative Agency of Neuro-Hypnotism. He believed that hypnotism was something that soothed the nerves and lulled them into sleep. His take on hypnotism was vastly different from those of the mesmerists. He believed that there were scientific reasoning and explanation behind what they believed was a supernatural force. James Braid ridiculed mesmerists especially when they believed that their patients developed powers like telepathy and telekinetic abilities. Braid was influenced by the ideologies of the Scottish Common Sense Realism who were also of the view that mesmerism was done through laws of psychology and philosophy instead of spiritual beliefs. Later on, Braid was regarded as a hypnotist in the true sense due to his take on hypnotism using physiology and psychology as opposed to the magnetists and mesmerists.

The mesmeric trance like state was attributed to a physiological process that came about with focus and concentration on a moving or fixed object. This concentration and focus that had to be done for a certain time put the person's mind to rest. The concentration caused a tiredness of the brain making the mind fall asleep, giving way to a trance like state.

James Braid formulated the term hypnotism from the Greek word that meant sleep because he believed that hypnotism came about as a form of sleep. Further research from his side concluded that it was not a variant of sleep and hence he sought to term it as monoideism. Monoideism is a process where a single idea or a dominant thought would put one into a trance. He believed that this trance was induced by focus rather than sleep. However, the term hypnotism stuck and was widely used. Neurypnology was the first book written on hypnotism and James Braid wrote it. However, after his death in 1860, the popularity of hypnotism in Britain fell and gained popularity in France. In France, extensive research was carried out in hypnotism. It was during this period that the works of Jean Martin Charcot and Hippolyte Bernheim gained massive popularity.

After Braid published his book on hypnotism, he began to receive several letters and reports that spoke about meditation techniques. He addressed these in several articles, which he titled as Magic, Mesmerism, Hypnotism, etc., Historically & Physiologically Considered. There were several parallelisms between meditation techniques applied by monks and hermits and his view of hypnotism. In his articles he threw light on the various similarities between the various spiritual meditations that was undertaken by the Hindus in India through yoga, other spiritual techniques from India and his views on hypnotism. He intended to incorporate meditation and extend the field of hypnotism and his interest peaked when he was introduced to ancient Persian documents and texts that threw light on the religious and spiritual practices of India. One such text was the 'School of Religions' from Persia.

In his text work Braid states that a person from Edinburgh who resided in India sent a letter in response to the book. In his letter he describes his thoughts and views on hypnotism, mesmerism and my beliefs. He also states that this stranger who wrote the letter described how similar Braid's view on hypnotism was to the ancient religious practices. He recommended the Persian text 'Dabistan' which spoke of meditation and how it seeks to have the desired effects. Upon reading this book, Braid found many of his beliefs and views overlapping with what was written in these texts. The saints and hermits also practiced hypnosis and carried it out in the way that Braid had stated in his book. The texts also threw light on the various benefits of meditation and self-hypnosis. However, the one thing that differentiated his style of writing and the writings and methods prescribed in the texts were that the text was of religious nature. Further reading of the Dabistan showed that hypnosis could be done by a person and did not require another person to do it. It could be done in solitude without the aid of a practitioner. Thus he drew conclusions from the book and derived that hypnosis especially self-hypnosis was really just a form of meditation rather than a form of magnetism and mesmerism.

He later prescribed in several of his personal accounts that people with ailments can go into a trance like state or get their nerves to go to sleep, without the aid of a medical practitioner or a hypnotist. They can do this by keeping their eye and focus on a particular point and collect the energy of their minds. Religious and spiritual Persians and Hindus have practiced this for several centuries. There is no requirement of any external being or force that will produce this state of mesmerism. Concentrating on an object will increase concentration and attention to details. The ideas of the person who performs self-hypnosis will get focused and he or she will achieve more clarity as he or she will be unconscious to any other distraction. No other lingering thought or no other distraction will make them break away.

Although there were several people who became fascinated by hypnosis and advocated the practices of hypnosis and self-hypnosis, there were also several criticisms of hypnosis. Several theologians believed that hypnosis was a dangerous act and when it wasn't practiced properly it would give rise to mental problems. It would make the person go mad and make the person lose their sense of reason. However, Saint Thomas Aquinas did not believe in this and claimed that hypnosis was not a sinful act. The loss of reason was not an act of defiance nor was it a deprivation of any kind when done with a reason. In 1846, decrees were issued from the Sacred Congregation of the Holy office, which claimed that it supported this form of practice when done for legitimate reasons. The decree stated that there is a lot of misconception and a lot of myths that are pertaining to hypnotism and when these were removed, it is simply a form that can be beneficial and when done in proper manner it would not cause problems.

The use of hypnosis was also found in the American Civil War. It was used for medical purposes and was proved to be very effective. It was during this period that a hypodermic needle came to existence. It was also used in combination of regular anesthetics like chloroform and ether. Though hypnosis was effective, several field doctors were apprehensive about using hypnosis to treat the soldiers.

Jean Martin Charcot was a French neurologist who advocated the use of hypnotism as a method to treat and cure hysteria. He started with what was known as 'The Numerical Method' that was based on several experiments and tests undertake in the field of hypnosis in several countries like Germany, France and Switzerland. In this time period there was also light thrown in post hypnosis. Research and several studies showed the positive link between hypnosis and memory enhancement. In this period it was believed that hypnosis attributed towards sensory acuity.

It was only in the 1880s that there was shift from the focus of hypnosis from being practiced for surgical procedure and inducing a painless relaxation without anesthetics by surgeons to those who dealt with mental health like psychologists and therapists. Though Charcot was the one who influenced this shift, it was his student Pierre Janet who continued with this. He prescribed a theory called Dissociation theory that dealt with segregating the mind and its thoughts under hypnosis. This would lead to obtaining skills and memories that are deeply situated in the subconscious. Janet's works primarily revolved around the subconscious and he came up with therapies that would integrate various parts of the mind.

Ambroise-Auguste Liébeault served as the founder of the Nancy School. He was also the first person to write on the importance of association between a subject who wants to get hypnotized and a person who was going to hypnotize them (hypnotizer). He propounded a suggestive format that dealt with suggestions and requests rather than orders and commands to induce hypnosis into the minds of the subjects. Hippolyte Bernheim who was considered a prominent figure supported this view. Bernheim also co founded the Nancy school which deal with hypnosis. The two of them brought an important role to this school by making it the place for hypnotherapeutic theory especially in the 19th century. Other accounts in the 19th century included those by a psychologist from America called William James who gave detailed description of hypnosis in his book Principles of Psychology.

There were also several congregations that came up as the popularity of hypnosis grew. One of the first ones was the First International Congress for Experimental and Therapeutic Hypnotism that was held in Paris in 1889. Prominent figures in the history of hypnotism and those who gave theoretical frameworks and developed theories on hypnotism served as participants. Important people included Hippolyte Bernheim, Ambroise-Auguste Liébeault, Jean-Martin Charcot and Sigmund Freud. Another meeting was subsequently held in 1900 in Paris. In 1892, The Annual Meeting of the BMA advocated the use of hypnosis as a form of therapy. In this meeting, the theory of animal magnetism or mesmerism was not given importance and hence was widely criticized. Though the BMA advocated the use of hypnosis for medical purposes, medical schools, universities and doctors refused to accept it as a form of treatment.

In the 20th century came several hypnotists with modernistic views of the practice. One of them was a French pharmacist named Emile Coué who also served as the founder of the New Nancy School. He proposed a new variant of hypnotism called conscious autosuggestion that was a form of self-help. He became widely acclaimed with this practice. Another psychiatrist from Germany Johannes Schultz merged the views of Emile Coué and Abbe Faria. He blended meditation found in yoga and conventional hypnosis and came up with a system called Autogenic training, which was a derivative of self hypnosis. An American Ukraine psychologist called Boris Sidis was the apprentice of William James at the Harvard University and came up with a law called law of suggestion. In this he propounded that human conscious splits and gets united. The subconscious and the conscious are split and the degree of this depends upon suggestibility. Gustave Le Bon founded crowd psychology in the 20th century. In this he formulated parallelism between the leader and the crowd. The leader acts as a hypnotist and his views influence his followers. This was a derivative of the suggestibility concept formulated by Boris Sidis.

Another contributor to the field of hypnotism was Sigmund Freud. In the end of the 19th century, hypnotism became widely practiced. Charcot popularized it and the public became more aware of it. This served as the base for the psychoanalysis by Sigmund Freud who was consequently the student of Charcot. He was also inspired by the many experiments that were carried out by Hippolyte Bernheim and Liébeault in Nancy School. With this he collaborated with Josef Breuer and formulated the abreaction therapy using hypnosis. He used this in his experiments and extended its use in psychiatry. This served as a platform several psychiatrists to use hypnotism.

Obstetric hypnosis, a form of hypnosis was extensively used in Russian medical practices. Platanov, a Russian medical practitioner became popular due to his extensive use of hypno-obstetric as a form of cure. This resulted in several cases of success, which caught the attention of Stalin. Stalin set up a nationwide program on this. It was presided over by Velvoski and merged the techniques of Pavlov in hypnosis along with the hypno-obstetric principles by Platanov. Other people like Fernand Lamaze extended the use of hypnosis. He visited Russia in the 19th century when hypnosis had taken up by a storm in Russia. He carried the ideology of painless childbirth to France wherein the process-combined reflexology inspired by hypnotic ideals and used psychological methods.

The 20th century also saw the advent of hypnosis and hypnotherapy in wars. In World War I, Korean Wars, World War II and other rebellion, it served as a base for the cure of neuroses. It was combined with principles of psychiatry and was extensively used to treat Post Traumatic Stress Disorder. It had a large number of success rates. William McDougall was psychologist from England who treated soldiers and the army from hypnosis. He treated problems like acute shocks and trauma. He also did not advocated Freudian theories especially aspects like abreaction that was a widely used concept in Freudian theory.

The British came up with an Act called the Hypnotism Act in 1952. This act provided protection against unethical conduct by hypnotizers. It aimed at regulating the actions of hypnotizers for entertainment purposes. The British Medical Association advocated hypnosis. In 1955, they supported the use of hypnotic principles for fields like hypnoanesthesia and psychoneuroses. It was used for management of pain especially in cases like surgery and childbirth. It was during this period that all physicians and medical practitioners were compelled to receive some basic training in hypnosis.

The study of hypnotism began in the 1920s and one of the pioneers of this was Clark Leonard Hull who was a psychologist from Yale University. He used statistics and combined it with analysis to study hypnotic phenomenon that was a result of several experiments. He recorded this in his work titled 'Hypnosis and Suggestibility'. His studies and experiments concluded that hypnosis and sleep were two very different aspects. In fact, hypnosis had no links with sleep and that there were many misconceptions about sleep and hypnosis. Clark Hull aimed at busting myths and eradicating misconceptions about hypnosis. He focused mainly on the benefits of hypnosis. His studies indicated that those who underwent hypnosis received an enhancement in their functioning; they were able to think clearly and focus better. Their cognitive responses also increased. All his experiments threw light on the significant reduction of pain after patients went into hypnotherapy and how they faced an improvement in their memory. Hull adopted a behavioral approach to hypnosis. His efforts showed that all these could also happen without hypnosis. When done with motivation, suggestion and encouragement, hypnosis happens to work far more effectively. Physical incapability and any changes in sensations could be tapped into psychologically.

Andrew Salter who introduced it to the American masses popularized Pavalovian method of hypnosis. This method aimed at contradiction, opposition and attack of conventional beliefs and principles. He combined principles of hypnosis with a technique called classical conditioning. This was inspired by Ivan Pavlov who also experimented with hypnotism and altered the state of mind of pigeons into "Cortical Inhibition".

Until the 20th century, the Roman Catholic Church banned hypnotism. It was only in the mid 20th century that Pope Pius XII gave the green signal for hypnotism. However, he stated that hypnosis could only be permitted for safe purposes like medical facilities and diagnoses. It can be used in medical treatments by medical professionals and can be used for childbirth but caution must be exercised. The Pope believed that hypnotism was something that should not be dabbled with unless known properly. Only ethical practices would be allowed and those with high sense of morality can practice it. If it is used as an anesthetic then the general rules that govern other forms of anesthetics apply to hypnotism. Similarly, the American Medical Association also approved hypnosis for medical purposes. This institution encouraged research and study on hypnosis and discouraged certain aspects of hypnosis that they believe were not fully explored and hence could cause problems. At this point even the American Psychological Association approved hypnosis and adopted it as a branch of psychology. After the Second World War, there were further studies that were done. Sarbin, Hilgard, Barber and Orne did contributions towards hypnotism. Stanford Scales were popularized in 1961. André Muller Weitzenhoffer and Ernest Hilgard formulated these as a scale to measure how susceptible people are to hypothesis. This scale was used to draw conclusions across different sex and age groups. Out of them, Hilgard pursued his studies and research on induced anesthesia, sensory deception and analgesia.

Harry Arons was a person who helped to popularize the use of hypnotism. He did this by starting professional courses and training in various cities of the US. Hundreds of doctors, psychiatrists and physiologists were trained through him. There were also training sessions that went on for a period of 40 years that trained people in the various uses of hypnosis. He also was one of the most influential people who managed to persuade the medical practitioners to use hypnosis and the five decades of experience in this field made him popular. It was for this reason that practitioners often flocked to his lectures and conferences. He became a member of the faculty of The National Academy of Medical Hypnosis and served as a writer, editor and publisher. He also acted as a consultant and allowed physicians, psychologists, psychotherapists and dentists to consult him and offered them medical advice relating to hypnosis. He also collaborated with several people like Ki Ho Kim, Harold Hansen and Samuel Martin to name a few. He served as an editor for Hypnosis Quarterly and published numerous books on hypnotism. Some of the most prominent works were 'Handbook of Professional Hypnosis' and 'New Master Course in Hypnotism'. He even advocated the use of hypnotism on criminals and published "Hypnosis in Criminal Investigation'. Arons who traveled extensively to popularize this practice trained Law enforcement agencies. Famous lawyers and attorneys were also trained under him. He served a mentor; teacher and guide that made the community accept him and accept hypnosis. He sought to branch hypnosis into new forms and increase its practice in trails and judicial systems. During his tenure he also founded the Association to Advance Ethical Hypnosis after he served as a director at the International Society for Professional Hypnosis.

More commonly was the propagation of hypnosis for medical purposes. Dave Elman was another person who propagated hypnosis for this reason. He trained dentists and physicians in the art of hypnotism though he wasn't a medical professional. He defined hypnotism and it is his definition that is still widely used. He introduced rapid inductions and today it is a widely used form of hypnotism. He also threw light on hypnotic coma. This period also saw several stage hypnotists and the development of hypnotherapist. One such person was Ormond McGill who also served as a dean for the American Hypnotists and published several papers.

Skills for Health, the Government's Sector Skills Council for the UK health industry published a particular book for hypnotherapy called National Occupational Standards for Hypnotherapy in the year 2002. Training and courses were given and there were even certificate courses and diplomas that were conferred by the Qualifications and Curriculum Authority. International conferences were also held and assessments were made and those who fared well received medals. In India, hypnotism has been used for over several decades. Recently in about 2003, The Ministry of Health & Family Welfare, Government of India stated in one of the letters that it issued that hypnotherapy can be utilized. It can be used to treat people however only for ethical purposes by a trained hypnotizer. These days it is used to cure pain from surgeries, childbirth, mental health and so on.

Chapter 4 – Types of Hypnotism

Now, we shall process further, for that we have learnt the basics about putting the subject into the hypnotic trance state, and learn new techniques.

James Braid's Eye Fixation Method:

The method, being one of the widely used is also called the Braidism. There has been quite a few variation made to this method to arrive at the current 'eye-fixation' methods, including the induction method used by the Stanford Hypnotic Susceptible Scale, aka SHSS, the commonly used research tool in hypnotic field.

As you look up without any head movement then you fix your focus on any part of what you see, you are experiencing hypnosis which could also be sleep inducing.

Looking up hurries and aggravates the fatigue of the eyes. Do not move your head backward at this stage as this aids the eyes and eliminates eye strain. Turn only the eyes but not your head in the same position as the neck.

If your eyes are steady in this position, you will not experience any major strain in your eyes and you will rather feel slumber some. As you are undergoing hypnosis, you will establish deep intensification as you lay eyes on one point.

To induce the subject vide the James Braid's method, take a catchy illuminated object, advisably a lancet case or similar, placed between the left thumb, fore and the middle finger. By holding the illuminated from about eight to ten inches from the eye in a position where the subject might possibly exert the greatest effort to fix his eye on the object. The hypnotist must make sure that the subject concentrates on and only on the object in his hand, in order to make the method work effectively.

It is indeed salient to make sure that the subject fathoms the fact that his co-operation is vital for the success of the treatment, for which he is to keep his concentration engraved on the object on the hypnotists' hand. When the object meticulously engulfs the subject, the following observations are made. The first notable change would be the contraction of the subject's pupils, for the reason of the consentient acclimatization of the eye and the contraction subtly becomes dilation. The hypnotist is now ready to remove the object from the subject's stare, replacing it with his own eyes. The subject is now likely expected to close his eyes, involuntary however so, indicating the subject's entrance into the hypnotic trance state.

There is every chance that the subject does not let you put him through the trance, attributing to his slip in concentration. In such cases, it is our responsibility that we make him understand the vitality of his engulfment into the object and to insist him to keep his eye fixed towards the object and nowhere else. But in general, the subject will got through the trance without any hindrance.

Arm Drop Method:

As the name speaks for itself, arm drop method of induction is a method in which the connection between the subject and hypnotist and the effectiveness is measured by the subject's conscious control over his own arm.

To start with, the subject is instructed to levitate his arm, above his head. Make sure the arm is not rested anywhere and can be brought down by littleness. Now the hypnotist might start suggesting to the subject, allowing him to enter the semi-conscious trance.

What a hypnotist must do in the process is a throbbing question. After making sure that the arm is well positioned, the hypnotist starts making his suggestions. We ask the subject, to fixate his eyes to one particular finger of the elevated arm. We then whisper to him, insisting on concentrating entirely on the finger. We might add psychological suggestions, as in to make him comfortable and light. As he concentrates on a specific finger on the arm, the subject might feel the other fingers black out. As he is entirely engulfed, his eyes fixed on his finger, the arm slowly lowers itself. We must note, that the lower the arm drops, the more closer the subject is to being hypnotized.

From the subject's perspective, the encounter is quite fascinating. The experience is one of a kind. As the subject concentrates keener and keener on the finger, the arm elevated as such, feels heavier and heavier.

But it is taken into consideration that, the hypnotist suggests what he sees rather what he anticipates or needs to happen. For instance, the hypnotist might suggest to the subject "Now you feel your arm lowering itself", because, he actually sees the arm dropping down, and not because he expects the arm to drop.

Arm Levitation method:

This way of induction requires not only the concentrated will of the subject, but also the carefully monitored speed at which he suggests to the subjects.

The ideal conversation, or the suggestions to be had with the subject are some like these, starting "As I count one to twenty five, a mild tickle like sensation is going to crawl up your left arm, letting itself travel all the way through it. You will feel your fingers fidget, unnoticed, involuntarily. Then, when you completely let go, rather than to control the feeling; when you entirely feel free, you will feel your arm rise above you. It will rise, above your body level, but not when you try to be self-conscious, not when you take control, only when you let go the inner most feelings in you!"

One thing to be tote in mind is that, a hypnotist can always insist, but never force the subject. It is important in this method that the celerity at which the hypnotist instructs to the subject. The hypnotist must proceed suggesting a point only after making sure that the subject has presumed the earlier said points.

Relaxation technique:

This is one of the commonly used methods. The prerequisites of the technique are almost nil, except the confidence you build in the subject's mind. The technique basically relies in the tone of voice and the words used by the hypnotist for the subject to be put into the induced state. Thus, the hypnotist must be soothing and comforting, rather being dominant and controlling. We, as hypnotist try to bring out the puddle emotions streamlined and pick up the one that needs to be attended to and for that, the subject must be convinced to let his guard down.

And you will not have his guard down, unless he trusts you. And to earn that, is the most important thing to do in this method of induction.

We, being hypnotists, might use a polite, yet confident tone to make him place his trust on us, not just consciously but also subconsciously. Tell him to relive all those convivial and mirthful memories and that he is slowly surrendering himself to his sub consciousness. When he is completely relaxed, we tell him that he must feel the breath and blood flowing through his body.

The method, treats the subject to be a passive participant to the process, that is, it lets the hypnotist do all the work and the subject merely listens and obliges him unconditionally. There is a technique that uses the relaxation, as a tool to hypnotize, but is slightly different from the previous one.

Instead of having the subject used as a passive participant, he is an active participant in this technique. Here, the hypnotist suggests that the subject that in his fully relaxed state, his extremities are soft and loose, limp and sloppy, similar to a cloth stuffed doll. Now raise their hand, suggesting them to let the entire adiposity of the arm cling along your fingers. After a while drop it, letting the subject feel a wave of relaxation all over his arm. Suggest him to proliferate the wave all across his physique, touching his body head to toe.

The process is repeated with the other hand, and the same hand continuously until he reaches the hypnotic trance. Though he is already in a tranquil state, he might experience the intensity of the relaxation increase steeply through this method. The above said two methods might as well be used as complementary, as in; using the first said method to have him relaxed and the second one to have him enter into the semi-conscious state of mind.

Staircase method:

Hypnotism, in its very core is the travel made along the fine line between the physical photoreceptors and the imaginary photoreceptors. The imaginary, or in other words, the mind's eyes are the ones that give shape to our imaginations and thoughts. Hypnosis, being a psychological science, appeals more to the whimsical view rather to the actual physical eyes. This method is one such appeal.

In the staircase method, as in every method, unruffled and placid concentration, that remains unadulterated from the external ambience. Here, the hypnotist calms down the subject, letting him relax, with his eyes closed. He then suggests the subject that he is going to count numerical values. He must also instruct the subject, that as he counts the numbers from higher to lower, he must picture himself descending from a set of stairs, and eventually when the hypnotist reaches the end of his counts, the subject is suggested to visualize himself falling flat into a bed or a pool, letting himself sink lower and lower into the bed or the pool.

This symbolically represents the mental state of the subject. When he is completely relaxed, the climbing down of the staircases sync with the process of digging deeper into the mind of the subject, wherein the first few steps of the staircase betokens the upper most, shallowest thoughts of the subject, whilst the last few steps embodiments the deep, inner most, hidden, long forgotten thoughts of the subject.

The subject is assumed to be completely in hypnotized; when he has reached the bottom of the quixotic pool he had put himself into.

Association Method:

This method is one among the widely used methods. And this is one among those methods that rely on the credence that the subject has, on the hypnotist and the credibility the hypnotist had built in the subconscious part of the subject. The soul of the technique lies on the solicited and meticulous efforts of the subject to follow the suggestions by the hypnotist. If at any point during or before the procedure, does the subject resists following the footsteps of the hypnotist, the results are definitely not fruitful. Thus it is also important that the hypnotist has a commanding yet subtle presence over the subject's subconscious. And again, careful that the hypnotist only has the presence and not the authority. Which in turn means, that the hypnotist can only direct or suggest what the subject might do and possible feel, and not compel, force, or oblige him to do or feel so, not for any reason but simply because, "It doesn't work that way". The below paragraph might shed light into the hypnotist's view on performing the association method.

Here, as hypnotist, we pull the subjects out of their consciousness, again, not against their will. We persuade them enter the hypnotic trance so that we could bring the long cloaked feelings that the subject has sought help unraveling. We do it; we dredge up those memories, dust them clean and find what the subject needs to do with those memories. If he wants to enhance those memories, if he wants them not to resurface again, if he is completely ignorant towards them; we unearth it all. But for that, it is of no avail that we communicate with the conscious self of the subject, because that is the one who seeks the help in the first place. So for that, we calm them down, luring them into the tranquility and seek the information within them. For which, the following are the quintessential conversation the hypnotist ought to have with the subject.

"Please place yourself comfortably." Encourage them to sit, lie or to be flattened as it pleases them. "Now, before you slip into the unconscious state, please hearken to what I have to say", Begin to instruct them, what not to do rather the to-dos so that they abide your words and ideas. "Please understand that you are here to let go and not to constrain yourself from letting loose. So consider yourself sleeping and do not curb your dreams. Accept them as they come, for what might help you. Never retaliate the feeling to let go. Drop the weights, for what bothers you." As you speak, you might as well notice the breathing pattern of the subject change to a less strained fashion and that is where they begin to enter the state of hypnotic induction, and that is where we as hypnotist unravel the reminiscence and help the subject with what they need.

Misdirection method:

What do you do with children who never want to listen to you? What if they won't budge for chocolates? What if they are not mature enough for books but not childish for toys? That is an extent to which some subject's subconscious can go up to. They not consciously, but subconsciously avoid or resist being hypnotized. What to do now?

Reverse psychology might be a colloquial term to describe it. Technically, we call it misdirection. That is, we take them completely of the idea of hypnotism and catch them off guard. That's right. When lowering the guard becomes complicated, completely making them forget about the guard at all.

For this method, you will need to keep them engaged, let them answer constant question of yours, keeping their mind busy. Ask them, if they could picture a scenario in their mind. Like, picture themselves swimming, driving or sitting in the porch and drinking tea. Now ask them to describe those imaginary situations, as in, if they had visualized themselves driving ask them if they could actually describe the road they are driving, ask them if they saw any trees along the sides, if they were driving alone or was anyone with them while they drive. Also ask them if they were the only one driving in the road and if not, ask them if they could describe the cars that were driving along and ask them if they could describe the interior of the car they were driving, like the color of the interiors and the side in which the steering was. We are more interested in diverting their attention from the idea of being hypnotized, but we must ask as many questions as possible.

If they had visualized themselves sitting in their porch, it would be easy for them answer the general question like the color of the house as it actually a routine for them to notice the color of the paint and it is better if we question them on the minute details, so that we keep the mind as engaged as possible. For instance, question if the neighbors had a mailbox, if there are no neighboring houses, question them what is there instead. In short, keep them almost engages to the very extent.

Once you're sure that they are not bothered about being hypnotized anymore, it is time for us to phase up. Tell them to try roll their eyeballs to concentrate and look into the darkness and concentrate in the middle of their brows, in the forehead, if necessary it even okay if you give a little tap or touch their forehead and help them concentrate better. Now tell them to try open their and without taking their eyes off the darkness, and they would feel their lids locking harder. The harder they try to open their eyelids, the tighter they lock. That is when you tell them to relax, to let the body feel limp and let them feel their own breath and blood flow. Apparently and eventually, they enter into the trance state.

Hypnosis for children:

Ever wonder why in the world would children need to be hypnotized? The following passages would help you to understand better. Basically, it is easier to stand on a mat, than to stand on a needle. And thus, the wider the experience, the less clumsy and riddled the mind id. And as children, as so confined to their smaller world, their minds are actually so tightly woven and is actually effort taking than the adult minds. The children do not conceive changes that easily as the adults do and so, you have to make them believe that there had been no change. There are a lot of problems, in that cute world of theirs. From bedwetting to mental traumas, there are a number of child problems for which there are no physical medicines. And that is why; they will be needing a hypnotic help. The methods and techniques are a bit liberal. We gently, soothingly carry them into the trance and make them feels so comfortable light. The method we use to hypnotize children is the "Bionic Arm Method".

The bionic arm method is the commonly used method for children. Take a guess at what children like? Stories! Yay! And yes, which is what we're going to do! Tell them the story of the 'Man who had a stiff arm!' It is not easy to suggest the little people, as they are not very interested in the Bionic Arm Method of Induction that helps the subject enter into the hypnotic trance state. They are interested in stories. So, we tell them about Bionic method, which we are interested in, through a story, which they are interested in.

First, ask if they know the story! They don't, but give the little fella sometime. When they respond, start talking to them, about the man who had this right arm. Tell them their right arm looks just like the man's! Tell, them, the man was just lying on a bed, comfortable and relaxed, just like they are now. Likewise, compare them to our fictional man, so that they put themselves in the position of the right-armed man.

Now tell them, that one fine day, his arm got stiff! As stiff as a baseball bat! Go in for the theatrics, they probably might love it! Tell them, the more they tried to loosen his arm, the stiffer it became. You might notice that children are trying to loosen up their arm too, but it's too tight to let free. Continue suggesting them that the arm has gotten stiffened further and further, and at one point, it totally goes lump and relax and a wave of relaxation flows through the arm. Feel their arm relax. Now tell them to radiate the wave throughout their body and get them extremely relaxed. Now tell them to visualize what bothers them, get them to explain it, and there we go! We have successfully hypnotized the big man!

The next big question:

Now, the next big question comes up! Does my child really need to be hypnotized?

There are several reason why the child might experience traumas like,

> - An unstable or unsafe environment
> - Separation from a parent
> - Serious illness
> - Intrusive medical procedures
> - Sexual, physical, or verbal abuse
> - Domestic violence
> - Neglect
> - Bullying

Children are light, fragile and immeasurably pure and strong. It is easy for them to be broken in the fragile side of them, but it is tough for us to know the reason they are broke as it is perfectly guarded in their stronger shell. A child never tells that he is being bullied, or he is having problems with sleeping habits. It is nearly impossible for us to figure it out for us, unless we penetrate into them, for which hypnotism is the best and only way.

Hypnosis can be highly effective for the treatment of various children's issues. Unlike adults, children are generally more receptive to hypnosis because they are much more suggestible. They have vivid imaginations that make it much easier to access the unconscious and bring about the desired change. As a result, hypnosis with children can bring about effective results very quickly. A hypnotist can use a variety of techniques with children including visualization, stories, puppets and role-playing.

Children are great candidates for hypnosis because they don't have the years of conditioning and resistance which adults have. Because they are used to learning they are often more receptive to trying something new, such as hypnosis. Children are not as prone to question the process. These things make it very easy for a hypnotist to work with them. Adults, on the other hand, are often wary and even reluctant and may have both conscious as well as unconscious resistance to being hypnotized. This doesn't mean they cannot be hypnotized, but it just may not happen quite as readily.

Hypnosis can be an effective treatment for a huge variety of problems, issues and disorders in children. Common ones include learning problems, academic performance, anxiety, bedwetting, self-esteem issues, homework struggles, thumb sucking, and fear of the dark. Also, coping with a traumatic event such as the death of parent or dealing with parents who are divorcing are challenges that can be helped with hypnosis. Children who struggle with frequent nightmares may benefit from hypnosis also. Hypnosis can also help children feel less anxious when facing a serious medical procedure such as surgery.

School is a significant area of difficulty for many children. Everything ranging from learning and homework to problems with peers can be addressed with hypnotherapy. Often only one or two sessions are required for effective results. Children can gain significant improvement in their self-confidence and ability to succeed with the help of hypnosis. Hypnosis can help them learn healthy and empowering coping techniques. It can help enhance and release their creativity also. With the help of a skilled hypnotist, a child can really blossom and become much more successful and happier.

Hypnosis for bedwetting has been shown to be quite effective with many children. Children who wet the bed often struggle with feelings of shame and embarrassment, and feel a significant lack of control. They often feel especially vulnerable and their self-esteem can suffer significantly if the problem is not addressed and resolved as quickly as possible. One of the reasons that hypnosis can be an effective treatment for this particular childhood issue is that the unconscious mind controls most of our bodily functions. Hypnosis accesses the unconscious and works by using a combination of suggestion and visualization to stop the bedwetting.

You can have your child listen to a hypnosis CD geared to treat bed-wetting. Or you can use some hypnosis techniques to help your child. It is often best to consult with a hypnotist first. Either approach can be effective in essentially reprogramming your child to handle the need to go to the bathroom while he is asleep just as he would when he is awake.

You can help your child relax by having him sit comfortably in a chair where it is quiet and there are no distractions. Keeping the lighting low is beneficial. You can help your child relax by having him close his eyes and take slow, deep breaths. Tell him to think about a particular object, or have him picture a place where he feels safe and happy. If your child is restless you need to have a lot of patience to allow him time to relax.

Once your child is very relaxed you can make some empowering, suggestive statements regarding the bedwetting. Suggestive statements that may be used to help with bedwetting could include "You can control your bladder through the night" and "You always wake up when you feel the need to go to the bathroom". After making these statements a few times you can bring your child back to a fully conscious and alert state. Having him count to ten is one way to do this. Talk to him about the session and let him share any thoughts or feelings.

Children are wonderfully receptive to hypnosis. It can be a very positive and empowering experience for them. Always be sure to choose a hypnotist who is both comfortable and skilled in working with children.

The taboo, that child hypnotization may be as bad as black magic. Again, we are not the pied pipers of Hamlin! We are professional psychological examiners. It is purely and fully safe to have your child hypnotized. Because, the best way to attend the problem is, to look into it immediately rather to let it grow deeper. A stitch in time saves nine! Likewise, you will have to attend your child's problem as a child himself, rather to attend it when it had already reached the untenable state, at found adult or adult stage. The problem that's bugging the child might as well result in permanent problems, such as lower self-esteem, stammering etc., so it is enlightening that we attend it sooner!

Chapter 5 – How to Hypnotize Someone

In this chapter we look at the technicalities on how to hypnotize someone. Hypnotizing someone is usually a part of magic shows and often we are fascinated by it. In this chapter, we will explore the way through which you can hypnotize someone. Hypnotism is often confused with spiritualism or is considered to be an aspect of the supernatural. This is not true. Hypnotism deals with mental strength and focusing that energy to obtain results.

1. Choosing the Subject

The first step in hypnotizing anybody is to find a person who is interested in getting hypnotized. If you are just starting out, it is imperative to find someone who is willing to get hypnotized. Ensure you tell the person you choose everything that you are going to do in detail. Gain the confidence of the person by communicating with them and making them comfortable. In the end of the day, they should be confident in your abilities and comfortable enough. They should also feel that they are in safe hands, as this will produce better results. When choosing someone, also choose someone who is patient and relaxed about the whole procedure. Do not try to hypnotize someone without their consent. Do not exercise your skills on people with disorders especially mental disorders. Hypnotism focuses on the mind and people with any mental illness could get aggravated leading to severe and complicated problems.

EXACT BLUEPRINT on How to Hypnotize Anyone, Including Yourself - Mind Control, Self-Hypnosis, and NLP

Most people have very skewed views on hypnotism. This is due to inadequate light that is thrown on this art form through mediums like fiction books, movies and TV shows. Hypnosis is actually a technique that is used to relax the minds of the people. It provides insightfulness and clarity to the person. It also reduces brain fog and eradicates stress that comes with pondering over problems in the subconscious. Hypnotism is actually something we undergo everyday. In fact, the term 'spacing out' is pretty much what hypnotism is all about and we go into these via dreams as well. It is important to tell the person you are going to hypnotize that they are not going to go into a sleep induced form or become unconscious. People who are hypnotized still have control over themselves and are not in someone else's control. Hypnosis has several benefits including reducing anxiety and increasing the metabolism. It makes the mind more powerful by making it more focused and sharp. It also increases concentration and is a relaxation technique. It is best to find out the reasons why your partner wants to get hypnotized. This will reduce ambiguity and you can comply with his or her request. It also gives you a chance to know them well and get an insight into their thought process. This makes it easier to get them into the trance like state.

Also make it a point to ask them about any prior experience that they have had with regards to hypnotism. Find out their opinions and views on this art as well. If they have been hypnotized before you can find out about how responsive they were and what makes them uncomfortable. You can avoid the things that they don't want to do and opt for alternate techniques. You can also gauge the partner and person you are dealing with. It is also easier to hypnotize someone who has been hypnotized before. Be sure to reassure your subject. They should trust you and believe in what you do. Guide them gently and be prepared to answer all of their questions.

Apart from choosing a subject to hypnotize, also choose a good location. The place that you choose must be free of distractions; it must be clean and quiet. It must also be comfortable. Remove distractive items like TVs, music systems and shut all windows if there is lots of noise. Switch off all phones and alarms. Close the door and ensure the lights are dim. It is important to note that the room should not be dingy and dark. Also ensure it is just you and your subjects. Let them sit in a comfortable position in a chair.

2. Ease Them into a Trance Like State

Make them feel comfortable and once they are in a comfortable position, ask them to close their eyes. Speak in a slow and calm voice. Keep your voice leveled and soothing. Drawl your sentences to make them sound smooth and talk like you are trying to calm someone. Speak softly and clearly. It is important to keep this soft mellow tone throughout the entire hypnosis session. Ask them to get into the zone by thinking of happy experiences. Alternately you can also start by asking them to imagine themselves in a peaceful location. A lush garden or a peaceful meadow or anything that is calming and serene. Talk like how you would talk to a child and make it a point to periodically reassure them. Request them rather than command them. Tell them that they are in control and that they are safe. Also give them their space and time to comply with your requests and suggestions. Ask them to relax and breathe deeply. Ask them to concentrate and focus on an aspect and breathe in and out deeply and slowly. Let them be in charge of their breathing. It is a good idea to also support them in this endeavor by matching their breathing to yours. Give clear-cut instructions for instance "Take a deep breath and hold it for a few seconds, now slowly let it out". Spend a moment or two on getting their breathing organized. This will give clarity and focus due to the high oxygen content that will go to the subject's brain.

If you prefer working with your subject with their eyes open, then simply ensure that they concentrate or focus on a particular point. Let them look and fix their gaze at either you or something else in the room. Wait for a moment until they are concentrating completely on the object. Make it a point to keep your gaze focused on them as well. This will let you know whether their concentration or focus is wavering. You can also offer guidance when they become distracted and gently bring them back to the stage of focus. Ask them to focus and pay attention. Tell them to also relax their eyelids.

When it comes to relaxing it is imperative that they relax their body part by part. Make sure they are calm and that they are breathing properly. Start by gently instructing them to relax their feet. Ask them to leave these muscles freely and relax them. From here keep moving upwards like their calves, their thighs, their torso, back, arms, shoulders, neck and finally face. When doing this keep your voice calm and gentle. Also do not rush them and give them ample time to relax. Speak encouraging words and give reassurance when need be. It is important that they are relaxed and that they are comfortable.

Keep an eye out on the subject's body language and their breathing. This will give you an insight to their mental condition. The goal at this stage is to ensure that your subject is completely relaxed. If they still seem stiff and uncertain, use soothing words, pleasant imagery and even use soothing songs to calm them. Look for any signs for fidgeting and twitching like darting of the eyes, wriggling of toes, tapping of fingers and so on. If they do have signs of these, then encourage them to get them to relax. Alternately you can also have pleasing fragrance like incense sticks that will help them reach the relaxed state a lot faster.

Once they are completely at ease and have relaxed, you can start by inducing thoughts. You can opt for using the 'hypnotic staircase' technique. This technique is a very popular technique that is often used by hypnotists and hypnotherapies. It enables one to get into the trance like state. Ask them to imagine themselves standing on top of a staircase. Then ask them to envision them walking down step by step. Each step will make them relax and they sink further into the trance like state. The subject will get more absorbed in himself or herself. Use a soothing, controlled voice for this purpose. Ask them to relax after each step by giving them clear instructions, for instance "You are on top of a long staircase, you are going to start walking down this staircase and with each step you are going to relax. Take the first step and you will feel your body relaxing, now slowly step down on the second step, you will feel your mind becoming calm." Ensure that they become perfectly relaxed and are a trance-induced state by the end of this exercise. You can also induce thoughts by making them walk into happy surroundings and a happy place. Give them more details and describe the scenarios well so that they can picture these in their mind's eye. Also enable them to imagine. As they slip further into the trace like state, ask them simple questions that are descriptive in nature. Ask them what color the flowers of the garden are, what color clothes they are wearing and so on. You will be able to picture what is happening in their mind through this exercise and after a point you will no longer just be asking questions but helping them to focus their imagination and create vivid colors and shapes. Also ask them what they are seeing around them and when you get good descriptive answers you know that they are in the trance like state.

At this point start to opt for a more commanding tone. Keep your voice light and soothing but once they have reached the trance like states make your voice more assertive and instructive. Instead of requesting start to command, opt to use words such as "Do this" instead of "Could you do this". At these points they will start responding to you and adhering to your words. They should be able to respond to what you are asking and carrying out tasks that you instruct them on. It is important to not question them on personal aspects or anything they wouldn't be comfortable sharing. Also when they are in the trance like state use positive and encouraging words to maintain that state. Keep a goal in mind and adhere to that goal. Be sure to provide positivity.

3. Have a Goal in Mind

Hypnotize someone with a good intention. Ensure you have a goal in mind. Chances are the person you are hypnotizing will remember what they were instructed to do or say. It is for this reason you shouldn't violate any ethical code. Ask them to do simple tasks and answer regular questions that they would be happy to answer even if they weren't hypnotized. Do not use hypnosis to prank someone. Hypnosis is an art form that is used for positive purposes. For instance, you can use hypnosis to reduce your subject's anxiety levels. You don't even have to instruct your subjects or make them carry out any task. Making them come into this trance like state is proven to reduce stress levels and give them clarity. This is because of the deep relaxation they feel when they are in this trance like state. Know that you can't fix any problem or solve anything but you can ease their tensions. If the subject has any particular problem then you can ask them to envision solutions. You can get them to solve their own problems instead of spoon-feeding them. For instance, if they are worried about their future, you can ask them to envision a brighter future; you can ask them simple questions that would induce solutions.

If they do have bigger problems and ones that you, as a beginner cannot solve, it is better to ask them to go to a specialist or go to a hypnotherapist. If they are suffering from severe addictions, mental trauma, self-esteem issues and so on, it is better to recommend them to a trained medical professional. If, however it is mild and you are trying to get them to stop something for instance, you are trying to get them to quit smoking. Then you can use encouraging words in the trance like state enabling them to quit smoking. Help them imagine a world without their addiction using positive words, good imagery and soothing tones. It is also a good idea to know the goal of the subject and why he or she wants to get hypnotized. You can modify your technique appropriately.

Hypnotherapy is a relaxing technique. It combines focus and relaxation for optimum results. You must note that hypnosis is not something that is done to fix problems. It is allowing the subject to muse over their problem and fix it in their own accord. You, as a hypnotist only serve as a medium towards this. Do not expect immediate results. It is a slow and steady process and can only be done with the willingness of your subject. Since it uses a lot of mind power and self-reflection and introspection, it is advisable to hypnotize someone with a balanced mind. If they require major help it is best to direct them to a professional.

4. Completing the Hypnosis

It is important to slowly take them out of their trance like state. Do not pronounce sudden movements and instructions. Let them slowly come out of the hypnotic state and become aware of the surrounding. The ideal way to do this is to tell them gently that you will count till a stipulated number after which they will be out of their trance like state. When doing this, give adequate pauses of at least a second between each count. This will induce awareness. Alternately you can guide them back upstairs with each step they take making them more aware. When doing this explain to them that they will get more pronounced and alert in a soothing manner. Give them time to settle down and focus their thoughts once they have woken up. Do not engage them in heavy conversation or ask them to do any exciting or exhausting tasks, this will lead to disorientation and brain fog.

When they seemed to have relaxed and become steady, you can opt for simple conversations. Be encouraging and tell them that they did well. Also discuss the hypnosis with them. Ask them their thoughts and opinions, how they felt, how the experience was and so on. This will help you understand your technique a lot better and you will be able to gauge your impact on a person. It will also give you an insight on the experience of the person and provide you with corrective measures and steps to make yourself better at hypnosis. Don't pressurize anybody and give them adequate time to collect their thoughts. Also if they want to be left alone, comply with their request. Be prepared to answer all their questions with an open mind.

5. Answer all Queries

You are likely to experience a huge volume of questions after you are done with the hypnosis. At this point it is best to answer them honestly. Be mentally prepared to answer all the questions and clarify any doubts. The subject is likely to have questions before and after the hypnosis is done. The main reason behind preparation is to gain the confidence and trust of the subject. If the person is reluctant and untrusting towards you then he or she will not respond positively or comply with your commands. The questions that you are likely to be asked and the possible answers you can give are discussed below.

• Is this all-safe?

Absolutely. In no way am I going to change you. You will not be forced into doing or saying anything you don't want to. You will be in charge and I will be your guide. You will experience focus and precision of your subconscious. You will experience relaxation and soothing sensation. It is perfectly safe and after it is done you will be back to the same person.

- What is your course of action?

It is very simple. I will request you to carry out some simple commands that you will comply with even when you are not in the trance like state. You have the power to refuse and reject anything I say or ask of you. You are in control of yourself and you will be able to come out of the trance like state by yourself. I will simply ask you to imagine or envision some scenes and ask you to narrate what you are seeing through your mind's eye.

- How does it feel to be hypnotized?

Hypnotism is something where you will get induced into a trance like state. This is very common especially when we sleep because dreams have the similar ability of making us go into this trance like state. Hypnosis will help you focus your thoughts, give you clarity and help you to relax your mind. It also increases your concentration and enhances brain metabolism. It is very similar to altering your consciousness when you watch a good TV show or hear a lovely musical piece. When you are so focused and into something you will view it from a different perspective. For instance, when you are watching a movie, you get so absorbed by it you start viewing it from a different perspective rather than just being a part of the audience. This is precisely how being hypnotized feels.

- Will you make me do things or say things that I don't want to?

No. When you are hypnotized you are still in control of yourself. Your personality or your mind doesn't get altered. You can reject anything you don't want to do and not respond if you don't want to answer something. You are in control of yourself and you wouldn't do anything that you don't normally do.

• What are some ways through which I can be more responsive?

The easiest way through which you can respond a lot better is through relaxing. You will be absorbed into yourself. You will be focusing a lot harder and explore the power of your subconscious. If you are willing to comply and if you are eager to experience it then you will respond a lot better. If you focus and relax and let yourself loose and allow the hypnotizer to guide you, then you will be able to experience the effects of hypnotism a lot better.

• Is it possible that there are cases where I don't want to come back?

The suggestions that the hypnotizer will give you and the various instructions are simply exercises for the mind. You are basically delving deeper into your own subconscious. You will be in control of yourself and responsible for your actions. Once the hypnotism session is over you will be more aware and you will return to normal state of mind. It is basically a state of deep relaxation and when this happens you might not want to come back but you can't do much in the hypnotic state. The hypnotizer will also try to bring you back. You can also be brought back by yourself during emergency cases.

• Are there cases where hypnotism will not work?

There are most certainly cases where hypnotism will take a longer time to work on some people but generally everybody can get hypnotized. Imagine instances where you are so absorbed in something that you don't hear what is happening around you, or imagining a situation where you will have to wake up early and managing to wake up the next day. All these are instances which show that there are so many hidden abilities that we can do with our brains and that it is powerful beyond measure. Some of us have managed to develop our minds and tune it into certain manner to help us go about our task. Usually people who haven't been hypnotized before have a hard time getting hypnotized due to enthusiasm, apprehension and other emotions that do not let them relax completely. However, if you focus and relax and let yourself be guided by the hypnotizer you will get hypnotized a lot sooner. If you also actively participate and follow instructions of the hypnotizer, you will be able to find success.

• If we only use our imagination in this task, how is it beneficial?

Hypnotism uses and channels your imagination into focusing and concentrating. It provides a platform for visualization and imagery. It makes your mind more creative as it exercises the brain and increases the efficiency of it. The mind is very strong as it controls every other part of our body, it is also the organ with which we think, make decisions and through proper training we can unleash our mental potential. Hypnotism enables us to achieve this.

Chapter 6 – Self-Hypnosis

Self-hypnotism is a tool for self-control and can be used to regulate your mental deviations, desires, urges and cravings. Besides the ones mentioned, it can further be used to gain control over your overall mental state. Let us start our journey without further ado.

Like all good things that come in parts, Self-hypnosis has three stages. It would be impractical to start any process from the wrong foot. Hence, the procedure for self-hypnotism has been meticulously divided into three essential stages. Starting off from the stage that comes first, we will see how you can prepare yourself for the daunting procedure. The second stage will be focusing on more practical aspects of the process while the last stage is all about the precautions and winding up steps that need to be taken so as to successfully perform a self-hypnosis session.

Stage I - Preparation

The start of your session should be simple and as basic as possible. A simple start always makes sure that you are not deviated from the prime goal of the process. It also ensures that nothing too complicated is attempted so as to keep you one directional and efficient.

So, what are the steps you can take so as to prepare yourself for a self-hypnosis process? Let's find out.

Clothing

Always go for clothes are not just simple but also loose. It is pretty difficult to pay attention to your mind when the tightened elastic of your brand new pair of pajamas is killing your blood circulation. Instead of formals or other clothes are hinder your blood flow, go for something like sweats or a loose short.

Temperature

Choose an environment that is neither too cold nor too hot. An excessively hot environment will sweat you out, thereby dehydrating you, making you run the risk of too much loss of water from your body. An extremely chilly room will affect you equally adversely as blood flow and other essentials of your body are marred. Select a temperature that's in the middle of both the extremes. You can take the help of air conditioners or room heaters to regulate the temperature to suit the standard temperature.

Place

After making sure that the clothes you are wearing and the temperature you will be in are up to the mark, it's time to move ahead to the place. Usually performed inside, most self-hypnosis subjects are advised to select a closed room for the procedure. Make sure there is no one else in the room you select, and shut the door before you start the session. The room you select should not be too bright in terms of light coming from the windows. Again, it should be preferred that the room is a bit bent towards the dark side.

Posture

One of the most important parts of hypnotism is not where or with whom you sit, but how you sit. Yes, it goes without saying that the ideal position for hypnosis is sitting and not lying down. Many subjects have been known to doze off while the procedure is still on hence we would advise you to prefer sitting to lying down. Choose a couch r a chair to set yourself for the session. Make sure no part of your body is crossed, especially your hands and legs.

Aloneness

The biggest enemy of any hypnosis session is disturbance. Make sure before you assume your posture on your chair, you switch off your phone, lock the doors and windows, shut down your computers and reset your alarm clocks. Your hypnosis session cannot be considered a success if you get interrupted by daily life disturbances. If you are expecting an urgent message or a call, get done with it before you sit for the session. Remember, this is that portion of the day when you take the time out for you. No one else, however significant, should be allowed to intervene in this sacred period of self-revelation.

Aims

It is very important that you always set a specific aim for your hypnosis. Some people might do it for getting rid of bad habits while others might prefer to just attain peace of mind. Whatever your aim be, specify it in your mind first before venturing into the self-hypnosis session. The specification of objectives is as vital as attainment of the same. Unless you have a particular aim in mind, you won't be able to focus on the cure that is supposed to help you.

Some of the most common objectives for self-hypnosis are:

➢ Quitting bad habits, people drink, smoke and gamble! A variety of bad habits can be discovered in the general population. To get rid of these habits, you could resort to self-hypnosis.

➢ Mental peace is the most sought after goal in today's life. Our lives have become so busy and complicated that frustration and mental harassment are bound to intervene in the stability of our minds. In such a scenario it becomes a supreme necessity to attain some sort of mental tranquility. Self-hypnosis is the answer.

➢ Some people want to just increase their brain's functioning. Your brain is like a newborn dog. If you train it from the start, it will learn quickly and will pay heed to you. Brain training is as important as anything else. Self-hypnosis is a great way to have access to the awesome ability of brain control.

➢ Clearly your mind is a great weapon. When put to wise use, it can yield great results. Its health decides your personality and attitude in life. Basically your overall development depends on how good your mind runs and reacts. Self-hypnosis helps your mind stay sharp and focused all the time thereby allowing you the chance to attain self-improvement without any yoga classes or meditation.

> ➤ The first stage of self-hypnosis revolves around preparing yourself, including your body and mind, for the exhaustive process of self-hypnosis. This stage should not be taken lightly otherwise it could lead to drastic backfiring. It is all about building your entire structure from the very first brick. Make sure you make the foundations strong and the fundamentals correct.

Now that we have learned the fundamentals, we may proceed.

Close your eyes

Closing your eyes has a soothing effect on you. You will realize that your eyes are the most functional part of your senses. It is your eyes that make you aware of your surroundings. When you shut them down, almost more than fifty percent of disturbance that you would have received is deviated to other places. The first step to any meditation related activity is closing the eyes. This not only regulates the light inflow but also prevents any sort of visual distraction from entering into your mind.

Drive away your thoughts

The most vital part of this stage and the entire session is this. When you start you will realize that despite all your teeth-grinding attempts, you are not able to completely get rid of thoughts; that despite you trying your best, one or two random thoughts keep wandering inside your mental arena; as if all the thoughts in the world have suddenly conspired against your state of mental nothingness. This is absolutely normal. Do not panic because you are incapable to drive away thoughts entirely. Try your best at first. If you fail, try again. Not everyone is a yogi to get success in such matters their first attempt.

Be Impartial

The best way to prevent thoughts from entering your mind is to become an impartial onlooker and not an enthusiastic judge. Understand that the more you react to your thoughts, the more they will trouble you by repeating themselves inside your mind. The key is to stand aside and observe your thoughts without giving a single remark regarding their character. For example, if there comes into your mind a thought of savoring a mouthwatering pizza, simply let it go. Make sure you have had your food before the session so that such a thought would not affect you in the least. This is called impartiality which is an efficient tool to block thoughts from interrupting.

An Alternative

If you find it difficult to not have any thought at all, you could make a pontoon your opposite wall and focus your mind on it. It need not be a point; it could be a smudge too. All you require is one good center of focus and you are good to go.

Stage II: Play the Tension

Identify the tension in your body parts. To do this, you must separate each body part from each other and make sure you feel the tension in each differently. Start from the toes, as they are the low most part of your body. Pay concrete attention to the part in focus and realize as the tension starts leaving it. Use your imagination as the tension travels from your toes, feet, calves, hips stomach, chest, and head and out of your surroundings. Let the tension release itself slowly but surely. Do not rush this step as it may defeat the very purpose of it.

Breathes

Again, a very important step; breathing can work wonders to your health and add sufficient contribution to your self-hypnosis sessions. When you breathe, your lungs contract and relax thereby providing you enough body heat and exercise to keep going. In a self-hypnosis session, it is vital that you relax yourself. Take deep yet slow breaths. With every intake of air you take, you can see positive energy entering your body. Likewise, every exhalation makes you notice the negativity leaving your body. You can work your imagination to suit your visual imagery. Picture the intake of air to be a light filled ball of sunshine and the outgoing air to be a dark cloud hovering over a helpless village; treating to ruin its crops.

Imagine:

Now that you are almost at the verge of falling into the trap of self-hypnosis, it's time you started falling deeper into the labyrinths of your own imagination. Try imagining you are at the top of your favorite tower. There is nothing below except a vast amount of space and then water. Now picture you have been gifted a pair of wings but you have never flown before so you are skeptical about going down. Calm yourself and take a leap of faith. Picture you are falling down; spreading your wings for the very first time ever in your life; this is the start of liberation.

Picture every minute detail of this scene using your imagination. Try to get into the depth of every detail. Are your wings brown, feathery and frail, or black like a raven's; strong and sturdy? Give yourself a new face and make the jump, without any fear in the whole wide world.

Get deeper

You have now taken the leap. There is of course, no coming back. But it is time you started advancing into the next stage; which is a better place to travel by your mind. The pool of water that you saw from the top of your mind tower is now nearing you. It's not gravity that is pulling you to it; you are there all by yourself; look aside! You have got wings!

Do you feel a floating sensation yet? By now, you are supposed to feel lighter than before. Gravity no longer works on you but instead there exists a sort of anti-gravity which none other than you control. You gradually become the master of your own actions. You start floating but the wings are under your manipulation.

Say

Hypnosis

We have reached such a stage from where some real game could be started. Pick a statement. This statement must be based on your goal. For example, you want to quit a bad habit like smoking. Your statement could go like "I am going to quit smoking." make it as simple as possible and adopt it into your mental radar.

After you have attained the above-mentioned floating sensation, you can start saying this statement in a loop. Adopt a gentle yet firm tone, and repeat the sentence five times in a minute, taking gaps in between. After a while, try increasing the frequency and say it ten and then twenty times in a minute. Keep doing this until you reach the count of thirty.

Walk out

Remember to never snap out of a self-hypnosis stage. If you suddenly decide to jump right out of a state of hypnotism, it could backfire on your mental health in many drastic ways. In order to end a self-hypnosis session, simply resume where you started. Last I remember, you were flying. Slowly descend to the building you flew from. Detach the wings from your arms and start walking down the steps. Make sure you walk slowly unless you trip. Mishaps occurring inside your minds could adversely affect you in reality as well. A smooth transition from hypnosis to reality should be preferred over a shocking snapping out.

Stage III: Enhancement

No self-hypnosis session will truly work if you do not have the required willpower to change or take control of your own life. Remember, hypnotism is only a tool while you are the real subject. Wake up every morning to repeat your statements in front of the mirror. Do not easily give in to urges that you vowed you would not be tempted by during your sessions. Quit the bad habits you swore you would.

Make sure after coming to reality you keep the promises you made while you were under hypnotism. Use your imagination to feel better about yourself. Whatever objective you are working towards, picture yourself getting it. Induce the much needed self-confidence and mental courage inside you so as to work harder towards achieving the goal so established.

Self-Hypnosis: James Braid Eye Fixation

Choose a comfortable spot and you must be in a relaxed state as you enter the next step.

As soon as you are comfortable with the chosen site, start an intensive focus. Do not change the direction of your eyes. It is during this situation that you will feel that the muscles around the eyes and the building up of the muscles to keep your eyes open also plus the eyelids included. Blinking may also be frequently felt. And the eyelids would start to feel drowsy. Just keep on staring at the chosen site and prevent your eyes from closing. Others experience unclear images and some would mention that has a cloudy effect on them. In situations such as this, this is a case to case basis for different persons.

You will then feel that your arms, legs, and eyelids are harder to control. Feel the impression you are feeling as your eyes are starting to become heavier and eventually close. Then, gradually close your eyelids and you will feel how relaxed you are. As you start feeling light, inhale deeply and experience the relaxation slowly entering the different parts of your body.

As the soothing effect oozes, take several deep inhalations to come out of this hypnotic phase. Start pressing your fingers and toes then gradually open your eyes.

Try to recall on the different trials in life and push to gather courage from this procedure to be able to survive from the struggles of everyday living.

Meditation and Self Hypnosis:

Both disciplines share many, almost identical, techniques, such as breathing and visualization exercises. For instance, the Progressive Muscle Relaxation technique is frequently used in both disciplines. This is where the subject focuses on one part of the body relaxing, before methodically moving down or up to the next part. Creative visualizations, such as imagining you are strolling past a quiet lake, are also used in both hypnosis and meditation. So what is the difference?

Meditation is commonly described as the absence of all thought. Practitioners aim to have a still mind, free from conscious thought. If any conscious thoughts in words enter your mind, you must find a way of making them disappear. Often repeating mantras or focusing on something such as the breathing or specific images can help accomplish this. (Here is a guide to further understand meditation.)

Hypnotherapy is aimed at a specific therapeutic outcome. This might be weight loss, quitting smoking, removing phobias etc. At the beginning of a hypnotherapy session, the hypnotherapist may employ some meditation-like techniques in order to quiet down the conscious part of the mind. Once the chattering conscious mind is still, they are then most able to give the subconscious part of the mind pre-agreed therapeutic suggestions.

So both a hypnosis session and a meditation session might lead you to a relaxing guided visualization on a calming tranquil beach, but a hypnosis session will then use this state of mind to suggest therapeutic change to the subconscious mind. The person meditating will receive their benefit purely from the stillness of mind and the relaxation they experience.

Chapter 7 – Sample Hypnotic Scripts

The main ingredient in hypnotizing people, whether others or yourself, is using the right words spoken the right way. In this chapter, I present to you several sample hypnotic scripts for various situations that you can use as is or as modified. If you want to do self-hypnosis, you can record yourself saying these scripts and listen to them at your most convenient time.

For hypnotic scripts 2 to 19, use the induction, deepening and awakening scripts from Script #1 to bring the subject to a hypnotic trance, bring him or her deeper into it and after using the scripts for suggestion, to bring him or her out, respectively.

Script #1: General Hypnosis

Induction (to bring subject into state of trance)

You will later start to feel an intense sleep-inducing condition. However, given that you may need to be awakened because of a situation that is necessary, there will be no problem in doing so because of the alertness and potentialities available. You may need to be in a very comfortable position, loosen up and with your eyes closed. This is an additional feeling of support. There is nothing you need to do. The essential factor is to focus on your inhaling and exhaling. Hold on your inhalation to later release it gradually to lighten up.

Keep on working on a series of gradual inhalation and exhalation then later releasing the breath gradually. Just keep on going like this.

As you go progress with the procedure, you will feel that you are fine and are doing well.

You do not have to have or do anything special or to be in a special and particular place in order to enter into a hypnotic stage. Continually remember good memories, and positive emotions while entering another hypnotic stage already.

Simply allow this course of action to take place, gather the thoughts inside of you and enjoy the feelings of what is going on inside your body and let it flow until it reacts to words.

Understand and recollect all actions in response to my words – how pleasing and excellent the understanding is.

Picture your breathing patterns going through the solar plexus. Subsequently, think of a color that you would bring you ease and relaxation this very minute. Allow these to flow everything in you, in your entirety, starting from your head down to your toes.

Let the muscles go and relax and turn soft and notice the response of your body giving you additional fulfillment of happiness, ease and pleasurable sensation that brings you away.

While this is happening, feel the unity of your body and mind where in your mind listens and goes along.

In this spellbinding immersion, you only keep in mind happy memories, thoughts, and pictures, the mind leads you to and this is where the body is as of the moment.

Deepening

Later, I would want you to create and see a wall in the eye of your mind. As you go about that process, you are bound to see the numbers from 20 down to 1 fall down one by one on the wall. You will remember them as cooperative and striking as I start to mention the number 20 going down to 1.

The numbers you may be seeing will no longer be in order because of my counting down as I near the number 1. The number becomes smaller in size and when I reach the number 15, you may think that the numbers have vanished as they become smaller and smaller. During this period, you are in the deepest and sensational revealing spell.

19 and 20 are falling lower and disappearing in sight.

18 becomes miniature in size as well further drifts away into the séance.

17 becoming smaller and then followed by 16. Upon reaching 15, the number has totally vanished and you can no longer locate it.

Post Hypnotic Command

As you awaken from the hypnosis, there are some significant behavior and its changes within yourself that you may notice like thumb sucking, nocturnal and daytime bruxism (grinding of teeth and clenching of jaw), nail biting, hair pulling, problem drinking, unhealthy eating patterns (intense cravings for and overeating sweet and junk foods), procrastination, nervous tics and smoking, among others.

If by chance, you may need assistance through hypnosis, you best thing to say is DEEP SLEEP or slumber and chances are, you are on your way to the spell, and even more deeper than the one you were in. Additionally, you would only have to do so by giving full attention to a hypnotic session, alone.

Awakening

By counting from 1 to 5 now, as you awake, you will have more leisure, readiness, and are fully aware of your consciousness. You will feel tremendous.

Firstly, you are gradually awakening. As the trance ends, you turn to be more self-reliant and are positive about life.

Secondly, you appreciate yourself more and are positive about everything in your life.

Thirdly, you have more belief and glow.

Three, you feel brighter and lighter now. In a few moments, you'll wake up feeling much more centered, happier and healthier than ever. You'll be full of vitality and energy.

Four, you're feeling increasingly more normal now – regular breathing, alertness and clear mind. You're feeling more and more re-energized. Get ready, here we come – you'll be wide-awake and alert on...

...five!!!

Script #2: For Alcoholism

You are definitely relaxed now, and because of this sensation by being so relaxed you feel free from all tensions, anxiety and fear. You have come to realize that you are more confident and are surer of yourself because you have taken the enormous first step toward helping yourself.

You undergo an inner capacity moving on to pass through any hindrance that may pass your way to block your contentment from your family, friends and other circles in your life.

You now possess that increased amount of self-discipline. You can now facing any impediment in a controlled, free, and easy mind set. They way you now think are more coherent and keen consistently.

Your faith and belief have expanded in almost every way and every day. It comes to realization that you want to run away from your former self by drinking or some other forms of turning away from the truth in taking the place of faith, toughness and self-discipline. Now, you have turned to a far greater degree and cam approach towards everything. You are on your way because you have all that you need in attaining a very positive result.

As you sink more into your deepest, all you can practically listen to is the sound of my voice. And as I am leading you to remove your drinking problem and which can be done in five ways. The first phase is for you to loosen up. This is the most straightforward step s to bring you in touch straight with your hypnotherapist. You should not let anything stand in the way of being at ease in its entirety...let you should let loose of things in your mind...let all of you loosen up altogether. Now that you have let yourself go as we now reach the second step: the awareness.

You should be made to understand what brought you to this trouble and how to be aware of it totally and wholly. You have to go back to history to understand what led you to this complication. Why was it rooted in you?

This may be caused by a number of factors. Though you must try to gauge the reason behind this...you may have been partly turned down...or there was a sad childhood or traumatic event or memory by someone in the family who has also had the same difficulty...or you were not given what you wanted when you were young and because of this, it had stuck in you and your disposition and it actually already totally became a part of you. As some alcoholics anonymous had recalled, it may be that a problematic father-figure was the source of the problem without specifically being mentioned. This may be as an inclusion to the alcoholic personal program, and as advised in their twelve-step remedy, that this factor, could be corrected when someone who is more superior can provide a cure.

If the inclusion of a father figure can effectively bring in a remedy to this, we can suspect that the origin of this alcohol dilemma is a weak father figure. Another variable cause of alcoholism which has been proven in more than 95% of cases is lack of ego. He is so hard on himself by remarking on so many weaknesses he may have or by blaming his failure on himself. And probably in his yesteryears, the alcoholic may have been actually physically knocked-out by a bully or another mean individual. This is the worst scenario in destroying someone's self-esteem. This is one of the ugly reasons when one is abused by another person. When sentiment is focused on by the brain this could lead to fathomless agitation. This should be totally being eliminated for the person to totally be free of this vice.

Loss of self-esteem is an obstacle that may be embedded in the mind with an extensive force in a present existing situation. A list of proposals for awareness is now being specified. For a start, you come to an understanding with the reason why you ended up as a dipsomaniac or alcoholic. What pushed you to acquire an unsuitable father symbol and why this fact does not contain any similar description of you? The father you have is not you, was never anywhere near like you or may never be one like you nor he can never be our God in Heaven. There may be similar or the same remark but in essence, there is a variation or contrast. There is a passage from the Bible that is worded somewhat like this. "Call no man your father on earth just for fear of that one thing that they might be confused." We are going to expound further on your lack of self-esteem and may result in your liking your person in all aspects. You may be taken aback to a greater degree as to what kind of pleasing personality you possess. And what you never you were.

Now is the best time to entirely improve and cultivate on yourself and do away with and clear you of any practice that you are now moving away on. Now that your break and rest are done and with the new perception. We are now to start with a fresh and mature pattern. This will make you undergo a new path on how to be a different you. You will no longer feel the need to find yourself holding or needing or craving for a bottle of liquor or beer. You will no longer feel the desire to quenching your thirst or issues. All these impressions will no longer take the better of you. These patterns and advices are now leading you to have a very intensive result for yourself. A fourth factor done in the hypnotherapy session of drinking is to refrain from the origin of alcoholism. This comprises the habit of withdrawal and toughening of the self-esteem.

The practice method is a part of sequences regarding the alcohol removal. Your self-esteem has been restored. This is a most vital way of addressing the alcoholics. And a very strong reason in dealing with you as an alcoholic. Now that alcohol has been removed from your system, there will no longer come a time when you would like to taste it because for you, alcohol does not taste good and will no longer attract you. You would never want to return to being an alcoholic. Your dependence on God has been re-established and your belief in your religion has re-surfaced. This proposal is the fifth point in the session is in the continuation of reminders and heightened regularly in your existence. You now sink gradually back in to the good path. Your alcoholic issue has disappeared in your mind, soul, and you are now in perfect shape of mind and body.

Script #3: Anger Management

Picture yourself in a position that you have been annoyed and lost your cool like in the past. This time you have a different approach to an irritating situation and you are relaxed and somehow your judgment is tranquil. There is no longer a need to get back at anyone.

You accept how people are by being who they are with their own set of pressing matters. You do not mind their difference in opinions. Other people's values are so because of how you value their opinion. There is no trace of anger in you because you are in command of your feelings and acceptance that getting mad will not do you good. You have decided to be positive in your approach. You are in control of your temperament. Your choice for positivity is in you now.

You allow yourself to see and understand the point of view of others. You give yourself the chance to approach situations differently and clearly. You are clear with your emotions.

(Analyze and observe what causes you to get angry and request the help of someone to picture a comparable case while remaining calm.)

Script #4: Wetting The Bed

You feel great when you awaken in the morning. You are energetic and itching to start at once.

There is also an ease in getting up at night, if need be. You are awake when you make visits to the bathroom and you know where you are. You know the right place where to pee and get back to bed the moment you are done with your visit to the toilet. You recall the things you did during the night.

There is no reason why you should wet in the bed. If you feel that you did, you hurriedly get up because you are aware of what is happening. But, if you fall hard asleep then there is no way that you would feel that you have peed in the bed.

You fell so hard in sleep that no one is to blame for your bed wetting. There is much satisfaction because you never have to experience that kind of situation as you are in control of the issue. You no longer bed wet because you are aware of what is going on.

Night after night your sleep is lighter and you have the need to go to the bathroom and remember it. You observe that you remember your dreams and feel good about it. You consider yourself lucky because you are at a point to understand yourself. Nothing is wrong with you psychologically and physically. Now your family appreciates you that all is well with you.

Script #5: Concentration

Altogether, you feel tremendous about yourself. Your convictions are similar to others. You know that you are loved and know how to love yourself and others. Now you have a whole amount of self-assurance and faith in oneself.

There is something that you are able to give. You are a total optimist and pessimism is not in your vocabulary anymore. There is no difficulty in imbibing positive reflections and excitement. At night, good dreams are due to rapid eye movement sleep. You awake every morning in a very typical collection of a very enlightened sleep.

You allow whatever will come to you for the day. You let it flow easily.

There is an ease of focus. When there is a difficulty in focusing, the best would be to inhale deeply and take a break. Things and routine no longer annoys you. Once you have done these, there is ease in focusing. It will then be easy to pay attention and focus.

Your priorities are now organized accordingly to what should come first and last. There is no need for any difficulty for everything to be working well. There is no longer the issue of being pressured into doing something. There is no longer an issue to think hard back because of the natural flow within.

Script #6: Becoming More Creative

You have become the substance of your individuality. You were placed on this earth as man and as a consequence of your aspirations to acquire more knowledge to develop and progress more. You have a goal with your existence. Allow your inner self connection with your consciousness and unlimited standard of your thoughts to reveal your undeveloped capability complete your life's predestination.

You are now working on your gifted potentials. The capacity on your awakening is gradually coming out and reinforcing in you as days pass. You are commanding your inner self to strengthen your ingenious power to materialize and be felt by you. The universe now proceeds to shower you with motivation and determination.

You are presently using the power gifted to you by the Divine Mind. You are exercising your vast mastery of your conscious mind. The enlightenment of the universe is now in you and you now have in your hands the limitless ability to tap the immortal insight. Your are now in control of power that you have never felt. You manipulate the gift you now possess and you are now a visionary.

Script #7: Overcoming Depression

As you go on to roam and move around, all the noise you hear begin to vanish. You are in now focus on what you hear most, my voice. There are three points in misery that I want you keep in mind. This is our discussion and all three points is, in all honesty, the utmost truth for you. The first factor is that prerogative for being here. You're not inferior to anyone and you're the child of the universe same as the trees and the stars. What is revealed to you is that our universe is what it must be. As long as you acknowledge that the universe is much, much bigger than anyone, you can experience a deep sense of peace. This is where the second point comes in.

This is why everyone in the universe is distressed, aside from calamities, we self impose despair on our person. This is now the second factor in our discussion. Our sentiments are exhibited via electrical and chemical balances in everyone's brains. Continued series of unhappiness is a cause of a chemical balance of the brain. In my professional experience, it has become routine for me to pinpoint if there will be a successful response if I administer medication immediately and can mostly identify who is successful even without the use of medication. Whatever method is administered, success in doing away with despair is imminent. When you regain a better feeling, you can do without despair but it has a reoccurrence in the future or at some point in time. There will be additional periods of good and bad moods alike before this can be totally eliminated from your system.

The third factor is related with time as well as the necessary requirement to go on living, not only for the present times, but also in the here and now, in this moment in time. The third factor is very at the moment's period. To illustrate, a day before you were all sad and gloomy. Your new day has emerged and this new day can be considered a new start. The new day is momentous while yesterday is no longer here and it cannot be brought back nor be re-lived. There is no way and it is senseless that we can return to what has already been done. We will not be able to progress because it is no longer viable. It is dead and is without meaning and worth. The best thing is to learn from our wrong doings and charge it to experience. And the make most of what we have learned from that experience.

When failure strikes you down and you are now filled with frustration and you are somewhat enveloped by discouragement. You often tell yourself that you would just need one break or possibility or a new change of bringing yourself to a favorable outcome. You may want to ponder on a passage written by Longfellow that goes this way: "Nor deem the irrevocable past as wholly waster, as wholly vain, if rising on its wrecks, at last, to something nobler we attain." Suddenly, you have this inclination within you. Something written by Walter Malone that says: ""They do me wrong who say I come no more, when once I knock and fail to find you in, for every day, I stand outside your door and bid you wake and rise, to fight again. Though deep in mire, ring not your hands and weep. I lend my aid to those who say, 'I can'. No shame-faced outcast ever sank so deep, but yet, might rise again and be a man." You read this carefully and it gives you the urge to rise up again and make it work this time.

Exasperation of failure influenced the gloominess that sank your day. Yet, another day will emerge that is full of excitement and motivation. You are thrilled with the novelty of supposition and objectives. You have acquired and grasped from yesterday certain facts and experiences that would support your determination and goals for today. If everyone of us would achieve some good points, some widespread aspects of the cosmos, more extensive and massive than man, each bigger than mankind. Living and existence go on whether it is accepted or not. The concept of life, which in its fullness initially brings us to individual involvement in the achievement of each and every goal. This goes on for every human being regardless if we accept it or not. As each passing day comes, we receive each day and struggle to do everything to achieve at least something for our purpose and praying and hoping that it goes on the way we planned it to happen. We should look at life in terms of where it's bringing us. You have to figure out what are the signs that should work for us for we have as we go on with our routine every day. What we need to know and what we need to work on. This is what life is all about. Obstacles are not too focused on because you should know how to deal with them and how it is to solve and get rid of them. You only have obstacles because you do not want to part from it and because this is what your mind focuses on. This should not be the case. Without obstacles, everything is positive and everything will work out for our good.

Your true self is that about what you remain constantly concerned about. The solution to your problem appears only when you change your line of thinking and let the problem out of your mind so your mind becomes free to tackle the problem at hand and works without any other preoccupation.

Therefore, you only need to chuck your depressions and decide that you want to lead a normal happy life. Adopt the good things in all situations while discarding the negative ones.

Your depression is the result of being unable to effectively flush out the negatives. This permits the negative aspects to effectively block the positive aspects of love and hope and truth.

Each day throws up new hurdles, providing fresh chances to assert yourself and accept the reality of hope, truth and love. To discard the feelings of helplessness or hopelessness, closely analyze the situations and your responses for they may be different than what you initially thought.

All situations are unique in their own ways and the problem is not the specific issues that crop up but it's your chosen response to these situations that makes all the difference. Threadbare analysis of the situations and your responses permits you to arrive at a conclusion on whether or not there was any wrong reasoning in your response.

The negativity of your thoughts and spontaneous responses results in feelings of depression. You'll soon realize that a slightly optimistic twist to your responses can make a world of difference.

The secret lies in coming up with carefully considered responses that prevent such negative results. the failure to turn those responses to your advantage leads to depression. Another example can be taken from the Biblical reference to Lot's wife who was compelled to look back even though she was forbidden to do so.

Similarly, you cannot just be crying over spilt milk; that is why depression kills so many. Hence, it can be deduced that rumination over past mistakes would eventually lead to depression. Therefore, the proper course of action is to live in the present without dwelling too much on the past. Proper thinking is the key to leading a wholesome life.

Retrospective repentance on failures can only do harm and the best courses of action to lead a happy life would be to enjoy all the positives and eliminating the negative responses to the situations of life, past or present.

Live in the present; enjoy the beauties of nature and happier aspects of daily life. Though each journey must begin with the first step, we must look forward to higher goals and accomplishments without worrying about the past. Dwelling on past misadventures or failures is only bound to delay further progress.

Look closely, lest this day pass without progress. This day is also meant to propel you further in our quest for hope, truth, love etc. But, again, that was yesterday. Just because you did something wrong yesterday does not mean you cannot turn over a new leaf. Be positive today; you will advance in your goals and your quest towards attaining that happiness and truth.

Every new day is another chance that you have to set the records and your thinking, straight. Yesterday's mistakes show you the alternative road to fulfillment. This is what you get through positive thinking – a feeling of happiness, accomplishment and the warmth of love. You also learn to think before you act. Each good act is bound to provide satisfaction and confidence and take you away from depression and negativity.

Fulfillment means that you realize that there is a specific plan for you and that life is a learning experience, each day at a time.

By replacing negative thoughts with positive thoughts, every new moment is a new opportunity, and as you accept this truth, you feel the warmth of truth and love and hope course through your heart, you relax completely, confident that there IS a plan for you, and that even though you can't understand, you must go through these learning experiences that you are going through, in order to satisfy that plan.

To gain control of your destiny, these learning experiences are like the steps of a ladder – they have to be experienced and overcome to reach the next higher level. The belief that at the end of a dark night is a bright day full of promises, is indeed an apt one.

The existence of the darkness lends the importance to the brightness of day. Hence, instead of having a pessimistic perspective on the negative aspects of yesterday, you can simply give it a more optimistic twist by saying "That was yesterday". Reallocating your sorrows properly would indeed lead to a brighter way of accepting the truth.

Thus, giving a positive bend to your thoughts and being generally positive would entail treating every day as a fresh opportunity and every morning as a fresh chance to learn and expand your thoughts and your lifestyle towards higher and better goals and happiness.

The big question is why? The simple answer would imply that you have simply kept aside your worries, your problems and all those negative thoughts. They no longer affect you since it was your reaction to them which was the problem and you are now looking forward to reacting positively, avoiding negative thoughts and reactions.

You are now in a new phase of your life where there are only positive thoughts, relaxation and comfort amidst the resolve that you will avoid the negative aspects while carrying on positively and doing your assigned part properly.

Script #8: Overcoming Drug Dependence

You continue to go deeper and deeper; relaxing in both mind and spirit while the relaxation takes over your body entirely; your senses slowly descend into a relaxed slumber that pulls you deeper with every deep breath.

I shall now explain to you the convalescent stage that's important for addressing the severe problem of drug addiction. You will observe that as we proceed further and further with the suggestions being provided by me, their effect becomes deeper and causes meaningful and thorough effects upon you. That your drug problem is a thing of the past has been comprehensively established; the most revealing aspect is that you know it too.

You are cured and completely so. You do not carry a longing for drugs in any way anymore. You do not yearn for them, you do not seek them nor do you need them. You are at a stage where you neither want them nor are a part of your life anymore. The best part is that you are proud because you emerged on top. You certainly are on top now. You don't have anything left to prove as you've done it already. You have established your maturity as an adult. You have proved that you can hold your own in society and that you can earn a livelihood.

You've proven that you are second to none; you can study, think, read, that you can be a competitive and effective human being in every way. But, much more important is the fact that you've battled and conquered one of the toughest habits successfully.

A drug problem is like an illness that's seemingly impossible to cure. Many others would not have been able to lick this problem at all. Yet, you have done it, and that shows that you have come out passing with flying colors.

Since you have proven yourself by kicking the drug habit and coming out on top as well as having emerged victorious in your battle against drugs, it would be in your own best interests to remain on top of it. Persevering with cure can be as important as getting the cure itself.

A doctor would never advise a person who is recovering pneumonia or tuberculosis to seek employment as a sand hog to avoid relapsing due to exposure to the cause of the disease. Similarly, there is concern for relapsing into drug addiction if a recuperating addict is exposed to the same drug infested environment that either caused or aggravated it.

As you are totally cured, you may go wherever you want and do anything that you wish. You may also be anything but though you are fully and irrevocably cured, you still need to be in a climate that's conducive for you to be active and effective, which is one that's free from drugs.

Since you have been cured, exposure to drugs does not pose any danger. But even if you're fully cured, it's in your best interests to minimize any possible risk for relapse by avoiding the same people and crowds associated with your previous addiction. You need to ensure zero probability of relapse by giving yourself time to convalesce. Time is the great healer that makes you strong. Each passing day helps you recuperate and provides you with more strength to help your body and mind recover. Time makes you stronger and stronger with each passing hour and day. Time equips your body and mind to withstand disease.

Dis-ease. One most important words for you because that precisely is what can happen. To hit the nail on the head, you are going to be extremely happy and contented and the reason is crystal clear: you have successfully kicked this problem totally and comprehensively. You have accomplished one hundred percent of what you set out to do. Therefore, you will completely avoid drugs like the plague. You will also religiously and totally avoid all such places where drugs are rampant and prevalent.

Developing stability in all aspects of life takes time. As such, it's vitally important that you have adequate time to establish complete stability in them. That is because it's what you really want to do and what you're going to be. In other words you are going to be stable, adequate, and effective. Your cure is permanent and it will stay that way.

Your cure is final and you are safe: Stable, Adequate, Final and Effective. These four enigmatic words are spelled by the initials "SAFE", which you'll memorize, remember and never ever forget.

You may never forget it! You are going to permanently memorize it and it will remain a permanent fixture in your mind. You will be safe and you're going to be safe. SAFE! Yes, SAFE.

- "S" stands for stable. You will be stable and will always remain so – much more stable than ever before in your life.

- "A" stands for adequate. You're going to be adequately SAFE. You'll also be adequate in every way, at all times. Nothing will be able to unsettle you.

- "F" stands for final. The finality of your cure and its permanence in every way is established.

- And "E" is the most important and essential of all because you will be effective. Stability and a permanent cure do not carry much meaning if you are not an effective and performing person whether in your personal life or in your career.

This is the most effective word. All aspects and areas of your life are "SAFE" and are the keys to your safety and happiness. It reflects what you are – SAFE. Now sleep gradually. Sleep peacefully and let that suggestion take complete control and have a beneficial effect upon your mind, body and spirit. Let your subconscious mind seal it away securely, never to be removed.

You are SAFE and adequately, finally and effectively stable. Safe to the core and whenever you have any difficulty whatsoever, depression troubles you or if you are bothered by anything, you will see that magical word "SAFE" right in front of your eyes. SAFE is the key that tells you to reinforce those suggestions over and over.

"SAFE" is the magical word which is going to replace all the ills and problems that you faced in the past because "SAFE" is going to be the solution. Drugs were never a solution neither for you, nor for anyone else. But now, they're gone and they are finished. This is the final and permanent cure. Now you will convalesce for a few months or for as long as you require. You will relax and recover in a climate – and I speak of a social and personal climate – where there is no room for drugs. And after you have convalesced, you'll be at your strongest and fittest mentally, physically and spiritually. You may go anywhere of your own free choice and do whatever you want.

But now, everything is as it should ideally be. You are in a state of convalescing from your bad dreams and experiences. You are totally and genuinely cured of all the ills that were plaguing you before. Your deep sleep is taking you down the path of recovery and you will soon be as new as you were born – reinvigorated, rejuvenated and fresh.

Now sleep peacefully and cherish the silence that I will provide because, during these upcoming moments of silence, all my suggestions will have their potent and wonderful effect on your mind, body and spirit. This tranquil period of silence begins now!

Script # 9: To Move On from Someone

The foremost thing that you need to erase a person from your active thoughts is to first make up your mind and arrive at a final conclusion that you are positive about your resolve to get this person's words and past actions off your mind. This would entail that you go over the negative aspects of your association with him or her and cast them away. You then, proceed to mentally discard this person from your thoughts.

To return to your feelings of joy and fulfillment, you will have to first detach yourself from the negative mental associations and ensure your life's aims are met. Soon, you will find that your mind becomes tranquil and calm leaving the undesirable memories of that person to melt away and finally go away.

You're an independent adult who is self sufficient and self reliant. You will soon realize the futility and needlessness of associating with this person. You do not require nor seek anyone who reminds you of unpleasant or negative situations or incidents. Once you've decided that, it's quite easy to discard the person or their thoughts and memories.

The undesirable memories of that person will no longer affect you since you are totally at peace with yourself and have detached from their thoughts, memories and mind. The unpleasant words and actions of other people that you've just discarded no longer affect you.

You are enveloped with the divine white healing light, which surrounds you and floods you with a sense of strength while imparting you with a relaxed feeling in mind, body and spirit.

You have been freed.

Script # 10: For Overcoming Examination Anxiety in Students

All information you have ever received is recorded. Taking an exam provides an opportunity for you to practice your recall. You're now completely prepared for exams.

The art of taking exams is knowing what your instructor wants. You now see very clearly what answers are desired. There is no confusion as to what are meant by exam questions when reading them. All questions are clearly stated.

You no longer become nervous when taking exams. At any time you feel you might become nervous, you simply take a deep breath and the nervousness will go away.

Script # 11: For Personal Success

You happen to be an accomplished performer, since you have achieved victories in your other endeavors. Your heroics are challenges that were easily surmounted by you. The only impediment in the past was a shortage in vision and imagination. You know your priorities and work towards achieving them. Your disciplined approach drives you to continuously work towards reaching the desired results. You use positive and beneficial thoughts to regulate your actions. You are eventually successful due to your sustained focus on your ultimate goals. The need to win propels you to the accomplishment of all your aims.

Script # 12: For Overcoming Insomnia

You will be well served if you think of yourself as being sponge-like, with stress being squeezed out of you as you inhale thrice "slumber now". Pay attention to me till the completion of your relaxing therapy and until slumber becomes immediate and smooth.

Since you need a completely restful night to get up in a refreshed state and full of energy, follow the same triple breath ritual while retiring and fully loosening your muscles. The completion of the triple breath ritual will leave you comfortable. That's right – repeat "slumber now" three times. Slumber will soon overwhelm you and you'll enjoy a very restful night. If awoken suddenly for any reason, slumber will return immediately. The necessity to rest enforces itself and you get complete rest.

Taking three slow breaths while trying to sleep can help cause your mind and body to relax. As such, this induces your body to move into a drowsy state that eventually transports you into a deep and natural sleep. As sleep overtakes you, you're in a relaxed, comfortable and cozy slumber that will greatly benefit both your mind and body and usher you into a state that refreshes your whole being. This will provide you a serene and cheerful feeling of contentment as you wake up. This beautiful sensation will rejuvenate your body and mind as well as gear you up to face the next day and its various challenges. "Sleep now" is your mantra – take 3 breaths and relax in order to enjoy a deeply relaxing and energizing sleep.

Let me now guide you though the fine rainbow colors for relaxing, which are:

- Red + Orange,
- Yellow + green,

- Blue color,

- Purple + Lavender, and

- White color.

When I move from one set of colors to the next, you will be gradually transported from your alert state into a naturally sound deep sleep. On reaching white, you'll be transported into the sublime world of a deep and very relaxed state of natural, normal sleep.

- Red + orange – Gradually, smoothly, slowly, calmly, and gently float and settle deeper into a comfortable slumber.

- Yellow + green – Your entire body and mind are now warmed up and all your nerves and muscles are un-frayed...relaxing with each passing moment. The warmth of deep and deeper slumber envelops you till you slip into a comfortable sleep.

- Blue Color - Your whole being feels light in relaxation, giving you a nice, happy feeling of warmth and comfort. This transports you into a smooth, natural slumber.

- Purple + lavender – Slumber – a very deep, smooth and healthy one – is beckoning your mind and body into its soft, cloudy folds. You find your whole being floating around and peacefully slipping into a deep and comfortable sleep. You feel as happy as a slumbering baby and continue to enjoy the soft bliss that only a healthy slumber can provide. You feel drowsier, and you slowly put off your gadget, then slip into a deep and comfortable rest the whole night.

- White color – As you're drifting into a calm slumber, you'll fall asleep. Keep your mind blank and sleep now. Rest now – slowly, smoothly.

Script # 13: For Overcoming Procrastination

Accepting the suggestions that I'll give here will seep deep into your subconscious with each session. These suggestions will build the castle of your thoughts and with strength and confidence to achieve, will resolve your personality together. The ultimate structure that you'll build will stand tall and strong to enable you to achieve more and more.

Your orientation towards success will be immediate and make you believe that nothing can deter you from succeeding in anything that you want to do. Your renewed confidence and enthusiasm will give you the desired results.

You will, out of your own free will, stop procrastinating. Your confidence in your abilities and your mature resolution to succeed will make you want to tackle tasks that you wouldn't take up before. Once you shed off your old attitudes, nervousness and reluctance will vanish, which will lead to a better and more organized response from you. And, once you continue conquering those old attitudes, reluctance and nervousness, your sense of accomplishment will rejuvenate you more and more for each task.

Your reluctance in doing a job forced you to procrastinate and delayed your actions but that was in the past. Now, a sense of urgency prompts you to realize that, whether unpleasant or not, the tasks at hand need to be done no matter what. Your worries and reluctance are things of the past.

With each day of accomplishment, satisfaction sets in. Hindrances and diversions will vanish as you tread the road to success unhindered by procrastination and equipped with an unprecedented maturity.

With each successful day, accomplishing your jobs become much easier and provides you with increasing happiness and satisfaction. The initial attention should go to the small and seemingly insignificant jobs that you considered as mere diversions until now. The quality of your work will continue to improve and you will be ready to face the more significant and vital jobs since the diversionary jobs are out of the way.

Your confidence in your abilities will peak and response to your new tasks will be faster and more precise. As such, believing that you'll continue doing great work will become natural and unconscious to you. The feeling of inadequacy normally associated with with a new job or doing something for the first time will no longer be there since you are sure of success. Once you start on a positive note, the results will come with ease and without much effort. The maturity of your approach will give you a higher sense of accomplishment, much more than what you set out to do. This feeling of satisfaction will empower you to successfully accomplish future tasks.

New jobs will not bother you but on the contrary, they will spur you to act immediately and do well and you'll become even more productive. The reaction will be immediate and you will desire to act as soon as possible. Procrastination will be a thing of the past and you will devise better and more efficient ways of accomplishing tasks, which will transform you into a "doer" rather than a "complainer". Nobody likes a person who simply passes on the problem to other people. People only like the ones who act on problems. And that's what you are now.

You will never again be hindered by unpleasant chores because they'll spur you to respond faster, enabling you to finish early. Then you'll derive sublime satisfaction as each goal is achieved.

Your increasing maturity and positive thinking make you increasingly pleased and proud of yourself. Your life will be more pleasant because you'll feel an inner peace upon realizing that you have accomplished your goals without delay as well as experiencing the feeling of freedom that makes your life simple and stress free. This realization will give you a sense of accomplishment and lead to a better work attitude and productivity.

You are not going to be fazed or afraid of new tasks. Not having handled new things before won't stop you. You will no longer worry about wasting your time procrastinating that you can't do or give your best in things expected of you. You will do things with the best of your ability with the potential to get even better. You believe in yourself that you are the best person to accomplish tasks. And with that, you start by doing it, and not just thinking.

You feel more at ease with yourself because you know you are at par with everyone and could even be better to some. You will regard new tasks as tests of how good you are and do them with eagerness, passion and sincerity. You will realize how much you've improved in what you are doing. All doubts you casted upon yourself before have already vanished and greater things are looking up for you.

You will realize that you have more time to share with your family, your friends and your work. You have more time to spend for things that you enjoy doing. You feel your life is more systematic and you are in control of it instead of it controlling you. Things accomplished are beautiful memories of how good you've become. Accomplishing tasks is that rewarding that you are looking forward for your next tasks. You feel more important now because you are more dependable as you've grown more mature. You feel more accountable as an adult and begin to have more reasons to be proud of yourself because you know you are better in organizing and controlling your life.

You find success in everything you do and accomplish. With enthusiasm, you accept appreciation of your newfound maturity from others because you know it is true.

Stay calm and enjoy the beauty of having choices. You are excited, happy and keen of being more successful in all areas of your life. As you grow more confident, you upgrade your skills, you achieve more and more everyday, you are able to bring in more sales, revenues, and make a living that you think and believe you deserve. You deserve to be rich and you can make it happen.

I will bring you back now to your normal state.

SCRIPT #14: Confidence in Public Speaking

You recognize that you are improving in your maturity and personality.

You are more conscious now of your strengths and abilities.

Hypnosis

You feel more confident to accomplish the goals you've set for yourself.

You are learning how to trust, appreciate, and reward yourself.

You are more composed and comfortable in dealing with circumstances.

You are looking deep inside you for the strength and wisdom to do things right.

All your words and actions are uttered and done with certainty and trust in yourself.

Your confidence enables you to raise your head high as you continue with your life.

You appreciate and find beauty in everything around you.

The respect you give to others and to yourself is reciprocated.

You trust your instincts and the decisions you make. You are authentic and reliable.

You move past every achievement to achieve more and greater things. People don't sense ill things about you and instead see the true goodness in your heart.

You're happiness and enthusiasm are infectious.

People don't have difficulty approaching and being friends with you.

You are trustworthy.

People know that everything with you is true.

It is very easy for you to create new bonds of friendship and meet interesting people.

You easily relate with others so that they feel the goodness in you as you feel the goodness in them. Words uttered and the smiles you display are evidence of the sincerity of your feelings toward others.

You enjoy dealing and relating with people that you want to accomplish things for them.

You know that people go to you because of your uniqueness and because they know you are happy with the way they accepted you.

You have that unique ability to effortlessly draw people towards you just like how magnets work on iron filings. You have that special personality, honor, and warmth to attract people.

Your imaginative thoughts make you a happy person that continuously affects others.

As time goes by, you feel you become more interesting as you are interested in others. You feel more loved as you also love others.

Accepting friendship and acquaintances offered to you is easy because you believe you deserve it.

You respect yourself and you know how important you are to others.

You are a people-person. You enjoy the company of others.

You exude confidence when talking to others, even with new acquaintances.

You are calm when you are with other people.

You enjoy sharing ideas with people.

Others sense your sincere liking of them and they reciprocate same feelings to you.

Everyone loves you.

Hypnosis

People give attention when you share your ideas.

Others like being with you even as you like being with them.

In front of everyone, you feel the sincere acceptance of others and this makes you want more to accomplish things for them.

You feel the friendliness and warmth from your audience.

You feel they believe what you are saying. You become interested in and want to accomplish things for them.

You like your audience that much that you feel there is a certain connection that binds you with each and every individual in your audience.

You don't have difficulty freely expressing yourself in front of other people. You are confident.

You're calm and you present your ideas in the best way you can – clear and direct.

Everyone understands and accepts your ideas.

You have a clear mind and you think quickly.

Your lips are supple as your mouth is tacky.

You breathe deep from your diaphragm.

Your hands are at ease.

Your actions are spontaneous and free.

You have no problem in sharing your thoughts as you create vivid images for your audience to understand the messages you want to convey.

You are very much in control of things.

The strength in your legs supports you.

You are at ease.

You speak confidently of your thoughts.

You speak freely and clearly of your feelings and don't have difficulty expressing the message you want to share to your audience, whether to a large or a small group of people.

As you start, you feel the acceptance and friendship offered by your audience.

As you start, you know their attention is directed towards you.

You are confident. You are calm.

As you start, you know everyone is listening intently to what you are saying. It makes you feel better and adds confidence to your work.

You spontaneously express yourself with your sheer skill and talent.

You enjoy what you are doing.

When new ideas come to your mind, you freely express them and include them in your discussions. You speak with such clarity and confidence.

You are an effective and powerful communicator.

People consult you on a number of topics because they know you can freely give your opinions in a clear and interesting manner.

How you do it, is a pure display of your talent and wits, which captivates and amazes everyone listening to you.

You know also how to listen to others and how to learn from them. You are open to the point of view of others.

You don't have difficulty expressing yourself positively, whenever possible.

Hypnosis

You are very easy to listen to. You speak with conviction and vibrancy.

Your mind works like a river, spontaneously flowing with powerful ideas.

You are pleasant to listen to. You are not imposing.

People are interested in what you want to share because of your liveliness and glee.

Others who want to interact with you can easily feel your goodness.

You are humble, asking questions when you don't comprehend things. You freely express your opinions whenever you are asked. You know when it is your time to share your thoughts.

People accept your opinions because of your sincerity, honesty, and because they know it is a well-thought idea. You speak with confidence and spontaneity, not afraid to express your feelings.

The smile that you radiate when it's not time for you to say something is an evidence of your compassion and honesty. You want to understand other people that you show them that they can freely share their views before you share yours.

You display a level of maturity and understanding wherein you are willing to do other things just to make others understand what you're saying.

When you are asked to facilitate an event, you are calm because you know you are in control of everything.

You radiate peace and a sense of self-assurance.

Your statements are clear and informative.

Everyone is impressed by your clear thoughts and enthusiasm to express them.

Your good control of what you are doing, wide vocabulary, confidence in yourself, and clarity of ideas enable you to make your audience listen intently.

Your very sharp and idyllic memory is a great advantage for you.

You inspire others to speak their thoughts well and express themselves more. You inspire them to speak freely of their ideas and opinions on things.

The ideas you've shared and you got from others are gradually being combined to make a good and permanent mark in your subconscious. The same mark will affect your daily life and how you deal with it. You are conscious of the meaning of things.

As I count from three down to one, I will say the word "personal success." Try to imagine the things that you think represent how you view success in your life. Use this time to discover what personal success means to you. Try to understand yourself and feel what personal success is. Get ready: three, two, one "personal success."

From now on, for every day that will pass in your life, you will discover and be aware of the beauty of being confident in you. Confidence is realizing that each day is an opportunity for you to achieve your personal goals, to achieve what personal success means to you. Each day represents one step towards understanding yourself, one step towards discovering solutions to your problems, one step towards developing and discovering the motivation that you need to become the best version of yourself.

Achieving this will mean a fuller and richer life for you – a life where you can freely express yourself.

Script #15: For Speed Reading

Imagine you are sitting at your desk, in the most comfortable couch, and you're reading. You read with ease, absorbing everything. You read at your own pace ensuring you retain the information from what you are reading.

Try seeing yourself reading at twice your normal reading rate. But even so, you still understand and absorb completely what you are reading. You didn't notice but you also became better in comprehending and retaining information.

You gave your eyes an opportunity to see beyond things, to see every bit of detail you can. You know in yourself that you are better and are able to understand things faster with the aid of your eyes. The human mind works on extreme levels we cannot normally imagine. You let your mind take in and understand things twice as fast as before.

The speed at which you read and understand things will continue to improve, also at a rate you don't expect. You allow yourself to be better.

From just words, you realize how to connect them and make sentences that make more meaning to you. You understand paragraphs that offer more information than mere sentences more quickly. You become better in all aspects of reading.

In everything you read, you realize your unending potential to improve and become better and faster every time. You understand yourself more.

Script # 16: For Greater Self Confidence or Overcoming Fear

You discover now a new sense of self-confidence in you. You are independent and determined. You have confidence in yourself that you know you can do anything. Because of your newfound self-confidence, you feel more secure with yourself. You're reborn, you're way better, and you're self-confident. In your actions and words and in how you think, you just show how confident you are. Your renewed self exudes self-confidence. You are self-reliant and are full of inner security. You are self confident in all aspects, internally and externally. You discover the confidence within you.

You become more positive in everything you do. Good things are not idealisms but they are realities for you. As you detach yourself from negativity, you feel and experience the beauty of life. You only now see the positive aspects of all the things happening in your life. You regard every experience as an opportunity for you to learn and enjoy, to discover yourself. The more you think positive, the more positive things happen in your life. You feel good in your whole being, mentally, spiritually, and physically. You're at peace with the universe, with yourself, with everyone and everything around you. And in each and every day that will pass, you will experience more good results to happen. And this is because of the positivity in the thoughts that you have about everything.

You admire and believe yourself more. You become more and more self-confident. You are happy, you are content with your life and look forward to new challenges, which you see as opportunities for you to better yourself, to prove to yourself that you can. You are more optimistic and accept challenges with enthusiasm. You show everyone the inner security that you have. For you, problems are mere opportunities.

You become more and more self-confident. You are persistent, composed, and focused at all times.

You leave blame, jealousy, guilt, anger, possessiveness, and all other fear-based emotions behind you. They are all part of your past self. You regard them as steps for you to achieve the future that you deserve. You are independent and you know that it is you who will write your destiny. It is you who will draw your own reality.

Your mind is like a glass of water, as you try to disturb it, it just makes ripples that eventually go back to its calm state. You stay relaxed, emotionally stable, and mentally alert at all times. You are confident and certain of everything. Nothing can distort you from the beautiful reality that you are creating. Negative thoughts have vanished. You do not worry about anything as you are self-confident and self secure.

Script # 17: For Overcoming the Smoking Habit

First of all, you should have realized by now the reasons behind your uncontrollable smoking habit. You do not feel the need to smoke at all. We will only focus on your habit pattern, the root cause of your problem.

Habits are easier changed than practicing them. Self-awareness is the first step of overcoming your bad habit. A mere sight of the cigarette, and the urge to at least hold it, are things that you should be very conscious about. If you try lighting it, and smell the aroma of the tobacco, you remember all the times that you've used it. You've used it over and over again but you don't know why. You've done it unconsciously, you don't really know what you are doing. That was before, now you understand more things. You understand more why you are doing it. It is no longer an unconscious habit. You know that there is really no need for you to practice smoking. You know that with certainty. Because you're aware of your bad habit, changing the practice will be easy and effortlessly done. You won't struggle and long for what you have done in the past. This will no longer be a guilty pleasure for you. You now feel annoyed by the mere smell of it. You feel disgusted as you imagine that you were once doing it. The idea of smoking bores you. You might opt to throw it without finishing the whole thing.

The taste of tobacco is not the same anymore. You choose not do it. You choose not to try it again. Your decision is final. You stop and throw all thoughts of you smoking again. This is it. You will not try it again, tomorrow, the next day, in the weeks and years to come. You will stop now. And it is final.

You made that one big leap of putting an end to your smoking. You are aware why you need to stop. Think again of the reason why. Be certain, clear your mind. Think about the good things that smoking has given you. Is there any? Now think of the problems it caused you. You're finally letting it go. In letting go of your habit, you let go of all the problems you've experienced with it: coughing, pain, difficulty breathing, and all the troubles with people who don't like it. You give up things you don't want in exchange for the good things that you like: sleep, joy, security, health, and rest.

Cigarettes will be a thing of the past. There is no need for you to buy them because there is no need for you to use them. Immediately, you stop buying cigarettes. When others give you cigarettes, you are aware and you know you don't need them. You throw them away. When you touch a cigarette, you immediately break it. The mere sight of cigarettes reminds you of all the bad things you will also leave behind by throwing away the bad habit. You also imagine all the good things in store for you now that you've given it up. You understand that you gain more good things in giving it up. It will be like a walk in the park for you to give up smoking, considering all the benefits you can have in letting it go. How easy it is to let go of things you don't like. And you don't like smoking.

You feel you've accomplished something and you feel proud about yourself. Since it was easy for you to give up smoking, it becomes easier to change also your other habits. More so, it is much easier for you to conquer challenges in your life. You have more reasons to be proud of. You are more and more self confident, assured, and independent.

You will record all of your progress from the beginning. In every single day, you will tell yourself how much you've benefited in abstaining from your habit. The longer the time that you abstained from your habit, the more fulfilled and happy you feel. You're encouraged to do more and are able to improve yourself so you can achieve many more successes in life. After some time, there will be no need for you to record as it no longer becomes part of your routine. There is no need for you to record because you know that never again will you hold and light that cigarette.

You realized that there is nothing more powerful than your mind and how you think. It is you saying "no" to tobacco. It is extremely easy for you because you're now firmer and know yourself more. You are patient, more patient than before. You persevere and you're determined. Nothing can go against your decision. Days will pass and everyday you will see success as you overcome all the urges you had before. Sooner, you will realize the importance of that feeling of success that you want to continue and increase.

To further put an end to your urges for nicotine, cut down on your intake of coffee and liquor. In a short span of time, all of the nicotine in your body will be gone. Every time you urinate, these chemicals leave your body permanently. Together with the nicotine, you also lose calcium in the process. Aid this by chewing calcium rich turns and Rolaids. You also lose sugar in the process, which makes you crave for more nicotine. Aid this by eating three oranges of pink grapefruits per day. Because nicotine, affects your nervous system, you will feel stressed at first. Use Vitamin B complex to manage this. Continue this for ten days. After four days, you will feel better as nicotine is already gone from your body. On the tenth day, you will feel much better as your blood gets new and clean oxygen from your lungs. All the poison you had before will be all gone.

Script # 18: For Improved Study Habits

As a child, you set your study habits and it's been like that since then. You don't feel the desire to change how you study as you see it to be effective. Now, you want to change the way you study. You want to improve how you study.

Changing a habit is easy. You don't notice you are starting to set a new study habit.

Now, you find it easier to focus on what you are studying. You find studying more interesting. You don't find studying boring. And if there are times that you become bored, you still continue with what you are doing. You are still concentrated on learning and retaining information.

You no longer skim through what you are studying. You try to absorb everything. You retain every bit of information in what you are studying. You no longer skip or block information from what you are studying. You are more disciplined now to organize your time and allot some time for studying. It is very easy for you to organize how you study in the most effective way.

You feel better because you no longer set aside studying. You now give it extra priority because you know how important it is. You enjoy your free time much more now because you no longer need to think of your academics. This can only be possible because you know you were already done with what you needed to do.

Script # 19: For Losing Excess Weight and Eating Healthy

As you go deeper into your relaxation, all the sounds slowly vanish. The only thing that you will hear is my voice. You listen intently and carefully to the recommendations that I will give to you. You want one thing to happen in your life, lose weight. But you are not only going to lose weight, but you will permanently shed off those excess fats that you have. This program is designed for you to lose those fats permanently and to have the lean body type that you wanted so long. You will also be more alert and vigorous in the process. Those extra weights will be forever removed. This means you will be renewed after this program. You will be a better person, not only physically but also mentally and emotionally. You will be leaner and you will develop a new eating habit. Aside from this new eating habit, you will be more contented and happy with your life, with yourself. You will give yourself more opportunities to be happier and healthier. You will eat in the way you are designed to eat, that is to eat only whenever there is a real need for you to eat, which is hunger – the physiological need to eat. You will start it now, but you will continue this for the rest of your life.

Before, you were eating way beyond your limit. You were eating way beyond what your body needs. The excess energy in the food you eat will be stored as fat. In order to lose weight and shed those fat off, you burn it to supply your body with the necessary energy required for optimal performance. You will eat less to use up the excess fat as your source of energy for the day. Later, when you are leaner, you will maintain your body by eating only the enough amount of food that contains the necessary amount of energy that you need to live the day. Right now, you will start to develop the habit of eating less than you're used to. We will not measure how much you will eat, for your needs may vary from day to day. Eating less to use up the stored fat will make the difference that you want to happen. This constraint will not cause any trouble as it will enable you to use up the fats stored in your body and eventually lose weight. You will reduce the amount that you will eat significantly. You will use the excess fat as your source of energy. Starting now, you will develop a new eating pattern, a pattern that you'll need to religiously follow.

Naturally, fat contains significantly high amounts of stored energy. So, even if you burn or use up a lot of energy in a day's time, you will only lose little amount of weight each day. Because of this, you expect that weight loss will be gradual. Anyway, it doesn't matter how long it will take you to lose weight as long as you still lose weight in the process. Big things start with small steps. As long as you continue the habit, you will certainly achieve the body that you desire. You should permanently choose to change for the better. What is important is that you are slowly changing for the better. Losing one to four pounds is ideal. When you lose your excess weight, it is already gone for good. You will become a renewed person. You embrace your new self. Just like a butterfly that slowly opens it cocoon, you slowly show others the better version of yourself. Someone that is healthier and more beautiful.

Relax and try to absorb all the recommendations. Open your eyes to unlimited possibilities of what can happen. The image is of better food to eat. The foods you like are still there, plenty and all around you. There's always enough for you. You will not worry about starving. For you, there's lots of food everywhere. You need not store food anymore as there's plenty of it everywhere. All kinds and varieties of food are available to you. Starting now, you will only consume the right food that your body needs, one step at a time. You are done with eating rolls of fats. Storing fat is unnecessary and there are more important things than eating fat. You suffer by eating these rolls of fat. Your heart and other organs can be affected. You are unhealthy with fat. It ruins and endangers you. There are a lot of choices around you. You no longer need to store up excess energy in your body as there are plenty of sources around you.

One part in your central brain is responsible of regulating the biochemistry of your body. It also controls the amount of fat you store in your body. The control is located in the hypothalamus of your brain. It is your hypothalamus that is responsible of controlling your weight and altering your body chemistry. Your subconscious can be influenced by hypnosis as it can control both your craving for food and storing them as fat.

Using hypnosis, I am sharing with you recommendations on how to alter your body chemistry to be able to break and use up your large storage of body fat and to prevent the regeneration of these unwanted body fats. You will want to lose and eliminate all of those excess unwanted fat. Use the fat and turn them into energy. Burn it. Remove it through your urine. Eliminate it through all the possible ways you can. Through your urine, through your bowels. The movement is fast and as you excrete it, you slowly remove it from your body. Your cells are free again from those unwanted fats. You burn it and excrete it.

Use the stored fat as your source of energy. Use that energy to become livelier. As you eliminate these excess fats, you will eat less than what you need for you know you have enough source of energy in your body. You do not replace this as you still have some of it for you to use. As you use them, they will forever be gone. Gone will be the days when you suffered from it. You will get rid of them just as your shopping cart overflowing with goods that you can no longer carry it. You need to let go of some. After this, you will be healthier and happier. There is no need for you to eat a lot. You will start eating less but you will become livelier and happier in your life. You will become more active. You feel better than ever. You lose the desire of eating more than what you can until you achieve your target body size. Then after that, you will only eat the right amount of calories that your body needs.

After changing your body chemistry, you'll feel more fulfilled and wonderful. Eating make more sense now. You exercise, drink enough liquids to make you healthier and maintain the body type that you like.

You are losing more and more weight as days pass. You are leaner and the shape of your body starts to improve. The unwanted fasts are slowly gone. You feel stronger and you feel more complete in your life. You are now more in control of your eating habits. You have images of how you will look like in the future – sexier and healthier.

Now relax and try to absorb all the recommendations until you've fully imbibed them all. From your mind to your body and your spirit, your subconscious tells your hypothalamus to alter the chemistry of your body. Your subconscious continuously monitors your hypothalamus to do what you desire it to do and to experience the change that you want. Let the control center of your appetite significantly reduce your craving so that you will be able to use your stored fat as source of energy. And in utilizing them, you slowly excrete and eliminate it. Remove all the unwanted fats.

Chapter 8 – Guided Imagery

Hypnosis, as said in the initial stages of this book, hypnosis is not always done by a person to another. There are ways that a person could hypnotize himself. Here, the person suggests himself, relaxes himself and gests hypnotized by himself. This method, where the subject is being suggested or instructed by himself, the subconscious part of him will have no problem or harm in accepting the suggestion made whatsoever, which makes the method the most effective one, as it is important in hypnosis that the subject and the hypnotist or the instructor place ample faith on themselves. Considering the fact that here, in this self-hypnosis, the hypnotist and the subject are one and the same, there will be no problem of faith! So this method is often chosen by many people who are seeking internal relaxation and are willing to convince themselves for a better future.

Self-hypnosis is nothing but the efforts put by one self to relax or calm themselves. Self-hypnosis is used extensively in modern hypnotherapy. It can take the form of hypnosis carried out by means of a learned routine. Hypnosis may help pain management, anxiety, and depression, sleep disorders, obesity, asthma, and skin conditions. When this practice is mastered, it can improve concentration, recall, enhance problem solving, alleviate headaches and even improve one's control of emotions. During self-hypnosis, a person is usually educated to repeat or whisper a word, repeatedly again and again to himself until his mind grows silent.

People who are trying to get out of a particular life style, people who are trying to adopt a new, improved habit are the most common users of this therapy. Alcoholics, people with eating disorder, people who are willing to leave the drugs past them will find this extremely useful and helping.

How to?

Now that you've learnt what is and what are all the benefits of self-hypnosis, you might as well learn the technique used for self-hypnosis.

To start the process you need to feel physically relaxed and comfortable. Sit, lie down flat on stomach, or lie on your back, however it pleases you. Try using a basic relaxation technique such as the one outlined on our Relaxation Techniques page. Find an object that you can focus your vision and attention on – ideally this object will involve you looking slightly upwards on the wall or ceiling in front of you. Clear your mind of all thoughts and just focus on your object. This is obviously quite hard to achieve but take your time to let thoughts leave you. Become aware of your eyes, think about your eyelids becoming heavy and slowly closing. Focus on your breathing as your eyes close, breathe deeply and evenly. Tell yourself that you will relax more every time you breathe out. Slow your breathing and let yourself relax deeper and deeper with every breath. Use your mind's eye to visualize a gentle up and down or sideways movement of an object. Perhaps the hand of a metronome or a pendulum – anything that has a regular, slow and steady swing. Watch the item sway backwards and forwards or up and down in your mind's eye. Softly, slowly and monotonously count down from ten in your head, saying I am relaxing after each number. '10 I am relaxing'... '9 I am relaxing' etc. You can even repeat the words of your comfort, like, your own religious belief. Believe and remind yourself that when you finish counting down you will have reached your hypnotic state. When you have reached your hypnotic state it is time to focus on the personal statements that you prepared. Focus on each statement – visualize it in your mind's eye, repeat it in your thoughts. Stay relaxed and focused. Relax and clear your mind once more before bringing yourself out of your hypnotic state. Slowly but increasingly energetically count up to 10. Reverse the process you used before when you counted down into your hypnotic state. Use some positive message between each number, as you count. '1, when I awake I will feel like I have had a full night's sleep' ... etc. When you reach 10 you will feel fully awake and revived! Slowly let your conscious mind catch up with the events of the day and continue feeling refreshed.

What is guided imagery?

One other technique in self-relaxation is Imagery. Guided imagery is a self-help or therapeutic intervention during which a person visualizes things suggested in order to create physiological and psychological healing. Guided imagery, as a method used in self-hypnosis helps you in the Reduce stress and improve health, Increase depth and speed of healing, enhance wellness, awaken self-awareness, improve self-respect, self-confidence, and self-esteem, optimize creativity, Inspire peak performance for you and your family.

Visualize a lemon. Picture you are holding the lemon in your hand. Visualize it clearly in your mind. You can see its color, feel its bumpy surface, and see the stem. Visualize that you drop it on a wooden table and hear the sound it makes. Visualize you have a very sharp knife and are cutting the lemon in two. See the cut surfaces glistening and notice that you have even cut one of the seeds in half. Now visualize a sparkling clean glass and squeeze the juice from one of those halves into the glass. See it run down the side of the glass.

Now picture that you are lifting the glass towards your face so you can smell the lemony flavor of the juice. Place the rim of the glass in your mouth and as you tilt the glass up, let the lemon juice flow down the side of the glass into your mouth. Taste the lemony taste. Taste the sourness of the juice as it flows over and around the sides of your tongue. Savor the tart flavor and notice the flow of saliva.

This is how Imagery works. The thoughts and images you hold in your mind all day have impacts at subconscious levels of the mind and can cause changes in your body, your behavior, your feelings, and you're thinking. And thorough this technique, we tend to change the thoughts and replace them pleasant ones. Not only does the guided imagery, visualization, and self-hypnosis help to create a new frame of mind and therefore experience of "reality" which sends a correspondingly different calming chemical message to the body, but also the process involves reinforcing positive thoughts or ideas and positive behavior changes or actions. The new beneficial self-statements and visualizations genuinely encourage, uplift, motivate, and energize; rather than discourage, feed pessimism and anxiousness, and reduce energy and initiative, as the negative ones had done.

Utilizing this tool and technique to reduce stress and enter a relaxed state enhances your immune system, reduces the negative impact of stressors on your body (including improving certain health problems), strengthens your ability to respond in a beneficial and constructive way to life's challenges, emotional stresses, physical and emotional demands - all because your body and mind's resources are no longer being drained by chronic and/or intense stress or tension. It is truly an empowering process: knowledge plus effective tools and the skills to use them gives your personal power to create change, solve problems, and accomplish what you strive for.

Chapter 9 – Benefits of Hypnosis

What is hypnotherapy?

Hypnotherapy is a treatment technique used by hypnotists practicing hypnosis to treat a subject's problem or concern. In this state there is more access to the subconscious mind where memory, habits, and emotions are stored allowing the hypnotist to help a subject achieve positive and long lasting changes in their lives.

Let us understand a bit about how the mechanism of hypnosis works and what its distinctive features are. As has been mentioned above, hypnosis is that state of mind from where you are most likely to respond to suggestions. Now, contrary to popular imagination and beliefs, hypnosis is not a state of unconsciousness. On the other hand, it is a state of extreme consciousness, maximum even if researchers are to be believed.

Hypnosis is a mental phenomenon. The therapies revolving around and based on hypnosis have a major advantage over other forms of treatments. While medicine consumption and doctor sessions may help a patient recover from life troubles, hypnosis doesn't require so much of hassle. All you have to do is sit quietly in the company of a hypnotic assistance and you are good to go. The best part about hypnosis is that it deals with everything mental and rarely requires any physical effort to be put in for it to succeed.

Hypnotherapy is a treatment modality with specific therapeutic aims and specific techniques utilized whilst the subject is in a state of hypnosis. When access to the Subconscious is gained through use of hypnosis, a more profound level of relaxation with a concomitant reduction in stress levels is achieved which aids in retrieval, resolution and re-education of old outdated memories, traumas, negative and distressing emotions, etc.

USE OF HYPNOSIS

The employments of Hypnosis are for all intents and purposes boundless in nature. The most widely recognized are weight and smoking control. It can likewise be utilized to liquor abuse, drug compulsion, stress, and different other mental issues, for example, sadness and impulse. Spellbinding can likewise be used to create memory, expand focus and enhance study propensities and test taking. It can likewise help enhance fearlessness and upgrade athletic capacities. Right away spellbinding is being utilized viably as a part of a wide range of settings, including instructive, therapeutic, dental and legitimate territories and in sales.

The differences between the art of hypnotism and other mental action lie in the features of hypnotism. In the section below we explore the various facets of hypnotism.

One of the most prominent features of hypnotism is that it deals with the mind and opens the gates of it. It enhances your mental stability and strength. You will be more focused and you will concentrate better. When you take a few moments to strategize and rethink of your decisions everyday you will be able to make better decisions. With mental enhancement comes the benefit of increasing your memory. The process of hypnotism works by getting rid of any unwanted distractions. It removes blocks in memories by filtering out your thoughts and makes information more accessible in our heads. With hypnosis you will be able to control your life a lot better. It prevents you from doing unnecessary tasks and breaks down your schedule to fit in only the important tasks. It reduces addiction of certain things. For instance, through hypnotism you can reduce the addiction to smoking. It also makes you more focused and goal oriented. The mind is trained to only focus on the necessities. You can control your reactions and responses due to increased in clarity. This will enhance your interpersonal skills.

With hypnosis you will be able to reduce bad habits and break addictions. These can range from mild addictions like coffee addictions or nail biting to severe addictions like smoking. There are many cases where the bad habits start to get restored. This is prevented by hypnotism. You can control your behavior and because of this you can keep the qualities that you like in yourself and discard those that you feel the need to change. Hypnotism is attributed towards positive transformation. It gives you a new direction and new perspective towards things. When combined with NLP you are able to broaden your horizons and make way for new experiences. With you being more in control, your self-esteem increases and you grow. As you get out of unhealthy habits and behavioral traits you will find better things to focus on. You stop thinking with your emotions and think practically instead. It keeps you healthy and happy. It also increases your problem solving skills.

Primary Ways to Use Hypnosis:

1. Hypnosis in Therapy

A session directed by a trance specialist and one customer. The main issue with hypnotherapy is that most states have very few if any laws overseeing the usage of entrancing in a remedial or clinical setting. To discover a confirmed individual in your general state contact the National Guild of Hypnotists, you will be given the names of a few guaranteed trance inducers in your general state. Contact those people and verify you are OK with the individual before setting up a session.

2. Group Hypnosis

Normally led in a gathering session with the end goal of:

A. A self-improvement session to chip away at taking off weight, quit smoking, learning self-spellbinding, and so on. Not as compelling as a one-on-one session, in any case, extensively less expensive.

B. Done in a configuration for stimulation purposes. Can be exceptionally compelling, as a fractionalization procedure is used, subsequently molding an individual to go more profound into mesmerizing all the more rapidly.

3. Self-Hypnosis

This is likely over an expanded span of time; a standout amongst the best approaches to use entrancing is ones close to home life. When a man takes in the self-hypnosis process he/she can keep on using it as a device to achieve numerous positive changes.

4. Hypnosis CDs and Downloads

This organization is compelling for those individuals who have a troublesome time creating self-Hypnosis aptitudes or does not have sufficient energy to chip away at the procedure. A CD or Download can be listened to at sleep time and is extremely compelling when utilized legitimately.

Why hypnotherapy? Hypnotherapy is one of the safest, quickest and most effective forms of treatment for the majority of psychological and emotional problems with few risks and side effects.

- Hypnotherapy fosters an attitude of independence and mastery in coping with problems and can also accelerate the healing process in many physiological problems.
- Positive aspects of hypnosis include the production of a much more profound level of relaxation with a concomitant reduction in stress levels.
- Doctors are becoming increasingly supportive of hypnotherapy as an aid to better health. It is a non-invasive therapy, complementary to orthodox medicine. The other vitals answering the question of 'Why' are below:

Mental Enrichment

Another brilliant feature of hypnosis is that it liberates your mental faculties. Do you take out ten minutes out of your daily life to think about things that matter to you? You will notice that you have been missing out on a lot of important things going on in your life. When you become a practitioner of hypnosis, your attention span will be enhanced and so will your memory.

Controlling your own life:

Why pull the strings of your life for someone else? The amount of control you will have over your life with the help of hypnosis is immense and unimaginable. Hypnosis will not only help you stop yourself from doing unwanted things but also show you the right way to do it. Bad habits are usually very difficult to let go of. Some sessions of hypnotism and you will no longer feel the urge to 'hold' on to your bad habits.

Quitting Bad Habits

Picture being able to dictate life on your own terms? Hypnosis is a great way to trim those bad habits that plague you throughout your day. A bad habit could range from biting nails to picking nose in the public and restoring back cruelly. All of us have our own set of bad habits that we would like to get rid of. Conquering bad habits is a herculean task. However, resorting to hypnotism is a good way out. You can pick what habits to keep and what to discard. In a nutshell, you become the master of your behavior.

Give your life a New Direction

As you gradually learn to master controlling your life, you will realize that are changing as a human being. You finally are at the doorsteps of 'transformation'. You are no longer a slave to your unhealthy urges and unnecessary desires that would have otherwise overtaken your senses had you been your usual self. Your life basically gets steered to a new and better direction with the steering wheel at your command and disposal. Hypnosis has always been connected with all things mental; however, few fail to recognize it as a means to achieve happiness that needn't be restricted to mental satisfaction. There are many physical forms of happiness too. Having regular sex, eating healthy food and sleeping at the right time to wake up at the appropriate time are all parts of your journey towards a renewed life.

The benefits of hypnotism cannot be put in words. Those mentioned above are only the main and core advantages of the therapy of hypnotism; the peripheral ones are numerous and too scattered to be made into bullet points and be presented. By now, you must have formed a rough idea about how hypnotism can help you transform your life and rejuvenate yourself. No amount of medication or meditation is going to help you achieve happiness and perfection like this. It is noteworthy to mention here that hypnosis is not a mere fantasy concept of marvel movies; it has become a very much real phenomenon and a really great tool for curing life troubles. Do you want to give it a shot? All you have to do is turn over to the next chapter that elucidates on how to perform or become a subject of hypnotism in the safest and coolest ways possible.

Problems that can be treated:

- ➢ Eating Disorders can be treated as well as problems associated with weight.
- ➢ Stress Disorders – In other words those problems of a health nature that can be treated by stress control

       – i.e. high blood pressure, anxiety, asthma and breathing problems.

➢ Panic attacks

➢ Gastrointestinal problems that are affected by a nervous disposition.

➢ Habits such as smoking and those that relate to addiction.

➢ Nail biting and nervous behavior

➢ Lack of Confidence that can relate to embarrassment both in the workplace and socially.

➢ Fears & Phobias: There are many phobias that affect people and these may not necessary be logical ones. People are afraid of all kinds of things.

➢ Psycho-sexual issues such as impotence or being worried about sexual performance.

➢ Speech impediments.

➢ Problems that relate to traumatic experiences and these can include unresolved issues arising from death, loss etc.

➢ Gynecological problems such as heavy periods, menopause trauma.

➢ Obstetric Uses: Helping women cope with the hormonal differences that occur during pregnancy as well as the mental issues that arise out of pregnancy.

➢ Study problems – People with a lack of confidence may fail exams even if they know their study work.

➢ Pain – Hypnosis can help people deal with long term pain management.

➢ Long term and serious illness management, such as in cases of AIDS, cancer and M.S.

Hypnosis

One has to appreciate the vital role that the mind has in being able to cope with all kinds of different situations. Look at the effect of placebos if you need to know how powerful the mind is. The suggestion used during clinical hypnotherapy introduces positivity and that helps tremendously in helping a patient to deal with their condition.

Chapter 10 - Hypnotherapy for Stressed Minds

Hypnosis can help reduce stress – Stress can cause serious illness in people like hypnosis-hypnotherapy heart disease, high blood pressure, obesity, diabetes, and sleep disorders. If you have a lot of stress in your life and your body is constantly in a high alert state then learning some simple relaxation, hypnosis and meditation techniques can change your life. If you feel like you can't get your stress levels under control by using diet, exercise and medicine then it's time to think about what hypnotherapy and hypnosis can do for you. Because Hypnosis involves putting you in a deep state of relaxation it gives your mind and body a chance to recuperate, repair and heal itself by experiencing the relaxation that it desperately needs. The good news is that Hypnosis can be used for stress management in two ways: First, you can use hypnosis to enter and enjoy a deeply relaxed state, throwing off tension and see things more clearly along with possible solutions to problems. This will help to prevent stress and anxiety. Second, hypnosis can also help you to achieve various healthy lifestyle changes that can reduce the amount of stress you encounter in your life.

Many people are reluctant to take medication to treat Anxiety because they don't want to become dependent on medication. Other people just can't seem to find a medication that works for them. Hypnosis is a drug free and very effective way to calm Anxiety and to treat the symptoms. By using hypnotic suggestions to eliminate the triggers of Anxiety people that suffer can sometimes find complete relief from those conditions by using Hypnosis.

Like meditation, hypnosis does require more focus and practice than techniques like simple exercise, hypnosis also requires some guidance, either from one self or with the help of a trained professional. Hypnosis may be a better option for those with physical limitations that make exercise more difficult. With Hypnosis there are no potential negative side effects. Also, few other techniques can offer such a wide variety of benefits. With consistent practice, virtually anyone can use hypnosis, and experience the many benefits this technique has to offer.

Facing your deepest fears:

Hypnosis has been shown to be an effective treatment for many individuals with phobias. A significant percentage of the population suffers from a phobia of one type or another. For some individuals it can be mildly distressing but manageable. For others it can be seriously debilitating. A phobia is an irrational fear of a particular stimulus. This stimulus can be a situation, a thing, or an activity. People with phobias will either go to great lengths to avoid whatever it is they fear, or they will tolerate it with considerable anxiety. For some people, a phobia can trigger panic attacks. In severe cases the phobia can end up literally controlling a person's life.

Hypnotherapy works by accessing the underlying cause of the phobia and eliminating the person's conditioned response to the stimulus. When hypnosis is used to treat a phobia, the initial goal of the hypnotherapist is to discover the initial event from which the phobia developed. The cause is often a traumatic event that occurred at an earlier time in the person's life. Often the phobic individual does not remember this event. It may be a memory that has been repressed for many years. Repression is a protective mechanism our mind utilizes by keeping memory of the trauma out of our conscious mind until we are ready and able to deal with it.

In order to access this memory, the individual will first need to be in an extremely relaxed state. The hypnotherapist will use techniques in order to help the person become very relaxed and focused. This state of heightened relaxation and focus is referred to as the hypnotic trance. It is during this state that the unconscious can be accessed. While in this trance state a person is very receptive to suggestion, which is what opens the door to bringing about the desired change.

Also, it is during this trance state that unconscious memories can be unlocked and brought to conscious awareness. The hypnotherapist does this by taking the person back to the place and time where the distressing event occurred. Addressing this old memory consciously will enable the individual to better understand it as well as begin to see it in a way that is no longer threatening. When this is achieved, the phobia will generally disappear.

This process is referred to as hypnotic regression. While it can be very effective it can also be problematic. There is a lot of controversy around this technique because if not done correctly or ethically, false memories can also be created. This has led to many legal issues when hypnosis is used with witnesses or defendants in lawsuits and there is a question of false memories due to hypnosis.

In many cases, however, this is not an issue and the phobic response can be dealt with very effectively using hypnosis. The hypnotherapist can help the individual visualize himself facing the feared object or situation without experiencing any anxiety. The hypnotherapist can guide the person in creating new thoughts and responses regarding whatever it is he previously feared.

The number of hypnosis sessions required for effectively dealing with phobias varies, and depends on several factors. These factors include how long the person has had the phobia, how severely the phobia affects him, the person's maturity, his personality structure, and how determined he is to be free from the phobia. In general, it will take approximately three or four hypnotherapy sessions. However, in severe cases it can take more.

If you suffer from a phobia it is definitely worth considering hypnosis as a means of treatment. While there are other methods that may also be effective, hypnosis may help you overcome the phobia, and in some cases even alleviate it altogether. However, if you do pursue hypnosis as a means of treatment, be sure that you work with a person is who has the appropriate training and experience. Also, be sure that you feel comfortable working with this person as trust is an essential element in any therapeutic relationship.

Anti- Depressant:

Many people find that they are depressed as a response to circumstances. Trauma can be triggered by events in life such as death, divorce or anything that impacts someone in a negative manner that renders them unable to cope.

In this day and age, the stressors that can lead to divorce are many and these can include moving to a new home or trying to get accustomed to a new circumstance, such as being a single parent bringing up kids without the help of a partner who has strayed. The world stops and people find they can no longer cope. That's when depression is liable to kick in.

Hypnosis
THE SIGNS AND SYMPTOMS OF DEPRESSION

There are many signs that give away a deep rooted depression that the hypnotist can recognize with experience. The mind is a complex system but some of these symptoms are ones that you can associate with depression.

Symptom 1 – People who find that they have no interest in their lives and don't even have the enthusiasm to get out of bed in the morning.

Symptom 2 – People look for physical ailments to explain why they are feeling bad. They are looking at physical problems because they don't want to face their depression and this side-racks them.

Symptom 3 – The patient is unable to stop binge eating or may just be failing at giving up smoking, drinking or drugs.

Symptom 4 – The patient may find that sleep is not possible because they stay awake and think about their depression, though be careful with this symptom. It may mean that the patient has a dependence upon sleeping medications.

Symptom 5 – The patient has a tendency to break into tears at the slightest thing.

The problem with recognizing the symptoms may be that the patient is taking anti-depressant medications, which their family doctor has given them. These mask the problem but do not deal with the root cause.

Similarly, patients may have been through the mill of trying to find relief for the misery rather than tackling the problems themselves because that's the only way that they can cope with the depression.

How to treat depression with hypnotherapy

A hypnotherapist doesn't deal with the part of the mind that thinks and speaks. He deals with the whole character and is able to glean what the true problems are from this interaction. Doctors, on the other hand, don't give this much time to patients and will merely treat symptoms in order to try and control the problem when the patient is not with the doctor.

The negative feelings that people feel would be coined as "business which is unfinished" by people such as Dr. Fritz. Imagine not being able to say goodbye to a loved one when he/she dies and you get those same negative feelings. These can include guilt, jealousy and a lot of other negative feelings and these are all triggers for depression. Why hypnosis works is that it copes with the unfinished business and allows the patient to finish it, so that there are not unresolved items going through the patient's mind all the time, making them unable to move on in their lives. Once they have tackled the subject, they find that they are able to move on and be productive again in their lives and that's important.

Clinical hypnotherapy uses a system of reinforcement of affirmations, which means that, not only is the patient helped through their traumatic experiences and dealing with them. They are also taught through these affirmations to be able to move on.

What happens when people are depressed is that they sabotage their own chances of recovery. Clinical hypnotherapy deals with this head on and teaches the individual behavior that is more positive, enabling them to overcome their fears and be able to see things in a different light. Hypnotherapy includes suggestion and suggestion is very powerful to the susceptible mind.

Many hypnotherapists use very powerful methods which are based upon psychological evaluation and advanced psychotherapy to replace negative elements within someone's life with more positive ones, allowing the patient – through positive suggestion - to be able to see things clearly from another perspective and to cope with the trauma that has happened to him/her in a much more positive manner.

Chapter 11 - Addiction Treatment Process

Hypnotherapy as a treatment for addiction comes along later in the rehabilitation process. The person seeking treatment needs to completely detoxify their system before they even consider undergoing treatment, and this usually means spending weeks or even months cleaning up. A medical professional offering hypnosis as a treatment for addiction is a hypnotist. This person guides the recovering alcoholic into a trance-like mental state in which the person is more susceptible to ideas and suggestions. In this state, those being hypnotized can become more imaginative and better at problem solving. In short, they're in prime position to sort out strategies for conquering their own addictive behaviors.

However, the only way that hypnosis can be effective as a treatment for addiction is if the person being hypnotized really wants to give up their destructive habits and behaviors. The treatment does not change minds or induce new outlooks. Instead, it helps to hone and refine a pre-existing mind-set.

It's important to understand that hypnosis is not a cure-all for addiction, but it can definitely serve a role in a comprehensive course of treatment. It's particularly useful in helping recovered alcoholics stay on the right track.

In order for hypnotherapy to serve a meaningful role in overcoming addiction, it is essential that the person receiving treatment be sober. Deep concentration is the cornerstone of hypnotism, and the toxins and dulling effects of alcohol limit the effectiveness of a hypnotic trance. Along these lines, hypnosis serves a greater role in preventing relapse than it does in quitting drinking. It serves as reinforcement, but not as a solution to addiction in itself.

After a person who has been struggling with an addiction to alcohol overcomes the initial hurdle of becoming sober, new sets of challenges emerge. At this point, staying sober is the goal, and doing so requires goal setting, plenty of focus and a healthy dose of optimism.

This is where hypnosis as a treatment for addiction really becomes effective. It allows the patient to get involved in the treatment process, letting them explore their own triggers for relapse and giving them tools to deconstruct a craving should one arise.

For sleep disorders:
Anxiety is considered one of the primary causes of insomnia. Hypnotherapy is considered one of the more effective solutions for sleep difficulties and is the utilization of hypnosis as a type of treatment typically intended for relieving pain or condition associated with a person's state of mind. There are many reasons that you have problems getting to sleep. Something might be on your mind and you are unable to switch off sufficiently from your daily activities to fall asleep at night. When you have experienced repeated difficulties dropping off to sleep, you might develop a fear of lying awake during the night. Stress and anxiety can keep you awake as well.

Misconceptions are plentiful regarding hypnosis, but, in reality, it is little more than a heightened state of consciousness whereby you are much more in touch with your unconscious mind than your conscious one. An illustration of this is watching water moving or fire crackling and losing awareness of the time. These, just like daydreaming, are natural trance states. Hypnotherapy may be used to deal with sleeping disorders as well as insomnia that have a tendency to originate from our inner thoughts and emotions playing out within our minds. If you ever have problems with insomnia, early waking, disturbed sleep or snoring, hypnotherapy could be beneficial to you. When you are sleeping, your conscious mind is still at work taking care of you. During hypnosis, the mind is free to forget about the stresses and strains of everyday living and relax. Hypnotherapy is able to directly access those issues, which are subconsciously bothering us. Take the time to relax your whole body and program your unconscious mind to help you to fall asleep much more quickly and easily every night. Hypnotherapy can assist with getting to sleep by -

Re-educating your mind to expect to enjoy a great night's sleep, teaching new relaxation techniques that allow your body and mind to slow down at the end of the day. Getting to sleep becomes less of a challenge in this state, helping you to discover techniques to eliminate some of the noise from a racing mind. Insomnia along with many other sleep problems is a very modern phenomenon and indicative of the pace of contemporary living and helping you to understand some of the causes of insomnia and sleep issues.

Hypnosis

Hypnotherapy has been shown to be beneficial in minimizing or eliminating the causes of problems manifesting during sleep. Typically, hypnotherapy subjects' sleep problems fall under two categories. The first is not being able to fall asleep at bedtime. The second involves waking up at an inconveniently early hour and not being able to fall asleep again. Mastering effective self-hypnosis skills will help you to significantly transform your sleep behaviors and can assist with indirect effects of insomnia and sleep problems like daytime anxiety and bruxism (teeth grinding during the night), sleepwalking, and bedwetting. By using hypnotherapy along with self-hypnosis, you can experience significantly enhanced sleep, mood, and energy. By learning to effectively utilize the techniques of self-hypnosis, you will take control of your sleep, mind, and body. You will be motivated by the recognition that the answer to overcoming insomnia exists inside of you. Consequently, you will increase your own self-confidence in your personal power as well as bolster your sense of self-esteem, which is essential to ultimate health and well being.

Chapter 12 – Hypnotize with Care

When you are hypnotizing people, it is important to use ethical guidelines and follow a set of moral standards. This is because you are playing around in the mind of someone else and you can do serious damage to their subconscious. Every word you say while someone is under hypnosis makes an impression that is deeper than any word that is said while they are fully alert.

Remember, humans only use a portion of their brain on daily basis. Some portions, even scientists are not sure what the capabilities are. Therefore, when you hypnotize a person, you are diving into the unknown, which can be extremely dangerous if you are not careful. This includes self-hypnotizing.

It is important to properly plan every session of hypnotizing and choose your words carefully. This will ensure that you do not do any permanent damage to yourself, or the person you are hypnotizing.

People Lie

One of the most important aspects of hypnotizing people is to realize that people lie. Whether they are lying intentionally or unintentionally, it is important to realize that they may or may not divulge all information that you ask for. Most people are not willing to admit in depth childhood trauma, which can become an extreme problem during the hypnosis process.

Make sure to have all of your subjects sign a waiver stating that you are not responsible should they have suffered through some child hood trauma that they may or may not remember.

If in Doubt, Do Not Hypnotize

If something doesn't feel right, or if a person does not seem to be completely honest about their experiences in the past, it is best to avoid hypnotizing them. This is because you can cause severe emotional trauma if you dig up old memories that they are not ready to face.

Many subjects are not aware of the power behind hypnosis, or the fact that it can land them in therapy for many years if they remember something that is unpleasant or traumatizing. In truth, if this happens, it is the fault of the hypnotist for not screening their client's better. Therefore, if you are the hypnotist and your subject experiences deep emotional trauma due to something you unknowingly dug up due to negligence, it is your fault and you should be held accountable for those actions.

Ensure that Your Subjects Are Mentally Strong

It is extremely important that you ensure that your subjects are mentally strong enough to withstand being hypnotized. This includes yourself. True hypnotists know that even a strong mind can be swayed and damaged. Therefore, a licensed therapist should only hypnotize anyone with psychological trauma. This is because they know how to control the situation should something traumatic arise and they can also close doors that are opened during the session.

Chapter 13: Neuro Linguistic Programming

Neuro Linguistic Programming is commonly abbreviated to NLP and was designed by Richard Bandle and John Grinder in the year 1970. NLP aims to awaken the potential that has been hidden away in the human mind. The mind is a powerful organ and can store huge amounts of data, information and knowledge. Today, the power of our minds is still unexplored though scientists are carrying out extensive research. Researchers and neurologists believe that through the development, training and channeling of our minds, we can achieve goals.

Some people have sharper minds than others. People are inherently one dimensional with a flair for certain aspects. There are several instances where the development of the mind can make people excel in several fields. There are many cases where people who are successful in their careers or professional lives lead stressful personal lives. They usually have little time and are isolated from relationships. Those who spend their time building their personal lives often have little time for professional endeavors. This is where NLP comes into play. It helps to channel the mind and train it in such a manner that every task that seems impossible can be done. It taps the unknown abilities of the mind. It does this through a simple process where in the neurons decode the thinking process that occurs in the mind and breaks it down into understandable bits in a comprehensible language. The mind then programs this language and creates an environment to do these tasks with precision and accuracy.

There is always a gap between what we think and what we do. The space between the accuracy of our thoughts and the corresponding course of action and execution leads to them getting jumbled. In fact, there are several instances where one would be planning something and this would not get executed properly. You might lack the skill, the time, the ability and so on that would render the task being more complicated than it actually is. It is in here where NLP is very useful. It guides our minds and trains our system to prioritize and think of appropriate course of action. It also helps in changing and altering our behaviors to respond better to conditions and situations that we don't have a control of. What we think and what we perceive are often not linked. Several times we end up taking the wrong course of action that makes us inefficient and ineffective. It is in these periods that NLP helps us to stabilize our thoughts. It gives us clarity and precision and lets us be better decision makers. These days we face a lot of distractions. The lack of time, busy schedules, narrow deadlines, etc. results in us incapable of completing tasks efficiently. We often lose focus and stray away due to this distraction. NLP reduces this.

Important Parameters of NLP

There are various parameters of NLP. These parameters or components must be understood to make NLP more efficient. These serve as the general framework or concept behind NLP. This section explores the constituents of NLP and the methodology of it.

Neurology:

Neurology throws light on how our mind works. There are two parts of the nervous system; this includes the central nervous system and the peripheral nervous system. Quick reflex actions and involuntary actions that don't require thinking like moving your hand from a hot vessel is attributed by the peripheral nervous system. The central nervous system essentially deals with analysis and thinking. It makes storing of data and information possible. It facilitates planning and decision-making.

The central nervous system does the thinking and execution by evaluating and analyzing a task or a situation. It then instructs the body to respond appropriately and creates the course of action to be followed. It is in this area that our thinking happens, thus ideas, judgments, perceptions are all stored here and makes us very different. This is why people can react very differently in the same situation. It is all based on our thinking ability and how our mind is channeled.

Similarly, perception also comes to existence. It is usually influenced by circumstances and experiences and these are stored in our minds. These come about by various situations and even our bringing. These are a direct reflection of our thoughts. It trains our mind in a certain manner and it is this training that is reflected on our reactions when new experiences happen to us. All these aspects are stored in our mind and facilitate our thinking and response.

Through NLP, storing important information and recalling this information is possible. It provides a base for better thinking and removes judgments and misconceptions. Wrong conceptions and bad perceptions are those that prevent us from growing and experiencing. These serve as distractions from our goals. Our genes also play a vital role in how we think. This is an aspect that cannot be altered.

Language:

Language is the second component of NLP. By language we mean it as a medium by which we present our views. It is a reflection of how we communicate and hence this can influence the way we perform and respond. Language is the connection between our thoughts and how we translate these thoughts into words. Processing a thought can be perceived very differently when it comes to speaking. This is why we should have proper communication channels. When our communication is improved there is little ambiguity and our thoughts effortlessly flow as speech.

Miscommunication is the harbinger of failed relationships. It is one of the most important causes of confusion and conflict. We often don't put the effort of thinking when we speak and we ourselves are unsure of what we want to communicate. There is clarity only when what we say and what we speak are the same. The efficiency of the mind can be tracked only when the message or idea is sent across precisely.

While we lay emphasis on speaking, our inner communication is as important as our outer communication. With development and enhancement of our inner communication we can perform better and are more motivated. It increases our abilities to perceive things and lays down facts before us. We also are able to decide better and it makes us more clear and precise. This will reduce ambiguity when we are trying to communicate. It also declutters our mind and segregates our thoughts and keeps only important aspects of the message.

Programming:

Programming aims at coordinating the mind and the linguistics so as to produce the effects of NLP. This means training of our minds and through this we able to control and exercise our minds. This increases our application to situations and circumstances. When our mind is trained well, our communication also improves and this is achieved through programming.

Programming deals with sorting our ideas and organizing them to reduce the clutter in our brain. These are essential for good functioning of the brain. If information is not well organized then it is very hard to retrieve information and there is an increase in the amount of distractions and negligible information. Programming also reduces the effect of emotions in our daily life. We often get frustrated and have periodic outbursts that can break our ties with people. Programming helps to harness this energy in more productive and positive ways in both personal and professional areas.

It allows us to be in control of our emotions and does not let our feelings influence our situations. This reduces interference and we are able to think with clarity. There is a lot of information that our brain processes every day and this could lead to information overload. This can lead to confusion if the vital bits are stored along with the information that is not needed. This will lead to poor focus, bad decision-making, and lack of clarity among other problems. Programming trains the mind to categorize information and separate the information overload into sizable chucks. It does this by getting rid of unwanted information and keeps only the important ones. This will increase our efficiency and our abilities to recall things. This also enhances memory.

In the above section we covered the three major components of NLP and how useful they are. There is still one major portion we are yet to cover. This portion defines the functionality of the system and throws light on how NLP influences us. In the section below we look at the levels of our mind and how NLP influences and moves across these layers.

The Three Levels of Mind:

Our mind has three major levels. These are termed as the conscious, subconscious and unconscious.

Through the conscious mind we are aware of our surroundings and we process information thorough this. This is where interpretation of information happens. When we interpret information, we break the information down into sizable bits and keep the ones we want and eradicate the ones we don't need. We also store this information for later use. When we are conscious, we are aware. Therefore, consciousness is a state of awareness. In the subconscious mind we store information and this information can be reached through proper training. The information is processed and sent to the subconscious that stores these without us being aware. The subconscious is very powerful and hence through proper training we can channel and apply our minds a lot better.

For instance, when we move to an area that is familiar, we do not put effort to understand the place it is a known surrounding. We don't pay specific attention nor do we focus on it too much. This is done without any estimation and calculation. This is attributed to the unconscious mind. The unconscious mind lets us do things without actually thinking about it. It is the place where we get instincts and gut feelings. The information is also stored in this part of the brain, however it is not accessible. Researchers are constantly trying to work out the uses of the unconscious brain. It is a fascinating part that enables us to make decisions won impulse. This is done from the data that is stored in the unconscious mind.

The main aim of NLP is to make the data stored in the unconscious parts of the mind more accessible. NLP is sought to present the data that is stored in there by gathering all information pertaining to a particular aspect. This is done by our past experiences and this data is tapped for impulsive decision-making. This information is also stored in the subconscious mind. It is believed that a person's intelligence depends upon the amount of information he or she can store in the conscious state of mind. Through NLP, we can access the subconscious and the unconscious parts of the mind and this will increase our intelligence. This also provides a good base for planning, forecasting, estimating and stabilizing.

Methodology of NLP

In this chapter, we explore the methodology of NLP. Through this we are able effectively implement NLP. The main concept of NLP lies in modalities. By this we imply that each information or experience that we have can be broken into smaller bits called modalities. These are comprised by emotional factors, visual factors, olfactory factors, etc. These comprise of both physical as well as emotional factors. All these modalities are also categorized into sub modalities based on the experience. For instance, if the modality is a sight or a visual form, then the sub modalities will include the color, the type, the shape and so on. All the modalities when come together form the experience or situation.

The main factor with which NLP plays on is modalities especially sub modalities. NLP aims at adjusting and altering these sub modalities in such a way so that our goals are met. We perceive our memories and experiences as they are. This leads to bias and judgments. When we alter the sub modalities of various situations we can trick the mind into perceiving these differently. These altered sub modalities of a particular experience or a situation can impact the way we function. It replaces the original experience and modifies our course of action accordingly.

Envision a stereo system; the stereo system is adjusted according to different facets like sound, frequency, genre and so on. Thus, the experience of the music will be different though the song remains the same. This is how NLP works. What appears to be a negative aspect can be altered to focus on the positive bits. These bits will impact us positively. In the following section we look at some aspects of NLP and how it will influence us.

•   Begin by analyzing your behavior. Seek to find patterns and trends in your behavior. NLP works by altering your behavior and with different behavior comes different training. Start by understanding your actions, you can only modify your course of action or response by knowing how you respond and what action you are trying to carry out. Give yourself different situations and write down how you react in each of those situations. Also, try to remember the actions that you do by sorting them through your brain. Try to understand yourself and when taking down notes make it a point to give yourself detailed structure. Look at the positive emotions and the negative emotions, the triggers that set of the response and so on. When you do this over a period of time over a lot of circumstances you will notice a pattern and have an insight on how your mind works. Break down the experience into modalities and break these into sub modalities and focus on the sub modalities. These sub modalities are what should get altered so that you can change your reactions. You need to make a note of these, as these are what make your mind inflexible and rigid. Getting rid of sub modalities and altering those in a positive way will make you more susceptible to changes.

•   After you have written down and made a mental note of all the sub modalities and how you want to influence them, you need to start comparing. For this purpose, you must have a comparison tool and it is with this that you will alter the sub modalities and change your actions and responses. Envision being in the shoes of another person. Think logically as to how they would react and respond to the same situations. Choose a person who would react a lot better than you and choose one who will react badly. Make columns and write down their reactions and their responses. Also chart out their prospective course of action. Alternately you can also ask two different people to write down and do what you are doing so that you get a more authentic feel and more precise information with regards to their response. Now compare and evaluate your action with theirs.

• Take your time to observe your actions along with the other people. Once you have a clear view of the shortcomings of your actions and your strengths, try to implement these in hour actions. Start by setting goals. NLP is goal oriented and therefore you can achieve more by keeping a target. Ensure you set a concrete measurable goal. It is important that you have clarity towards the goal; you should know what you want. If you don't, you will not get the desired results, as the mind will not be focused. You will also confuse your brain. There will also be an influx of information that is not required and this will clutter your mind. Have a goal and ensure that you work towards this goal.

• Once you have set your goal, the next step is to plan. Chart out the course of action that you will take based on the behavior pattern that you observed in your study. Realize that there is a lot of difference in how two people will achieve the goal. This is a direct consequence of the way our brains have been trained. This is what gives us our individuality and personality. This difference is one of the many things that we would be dealing with in NLP. Once you have charted out the course of action you would like to take compare the course of action with that of the other two people whose behavior pattern you recorded. At this stage, estimate the positive and the negative aspects and points of your course of action. Modify this course of action based on the way you would like to achieve your target. Also remember to keep track of the various alterations that you are making. Compare the altered sub modalities with the previous ones and keep fine-tuning till you are happy with it. Follow this course of action and record how the course of action impacts you. The goal here is to not seek perfection but get rid of clutter and free your thoughts from past experiences that can hamper your goal achievement.

• Now you would have launched NLP. Keep tracking your progress as often as you can and keep trying to modify your course of action. Note that you will not be able to achieve success at the very beginning. NLP is the training of the brain and this will take time depending on the differences in your behavioral pattern and how you actually want to go about the task. Keep a record of all the success and failures that you encounter as you progress with the NLP. This will give you an insight on your weakness and your strengths. Knowing your weakness will have a positive effect because it will let you modify these weaknesses. You will be fine-tuning your methods and you will be able to achieve success. With constant implementation of NLP, the type of training will become a part of your system.

• Finally you would come to the end of the NLP training. In this step you need to make your plans flexible. Keep a target in mind but be flexible about the various routes you will take to achieve that target. If possible, write down the various ways through which you can achieve your goal and highlight the strengths and weakness of each course of action. This will enable you to take the best course of action automatically. Don't over modify your thoughts. Keep refining them instead. The goal isn't perfection. Also modify those that have a negative impact, don't modify every tiny detail. Sometimes it ends up becoming redundant if you modify everything. They will also consume energy and sap efficiency. Stick to following a good plan and ensure that your plan is flexible. The key lies in execution. Keep incorporating changes and alterations but don't get too focused on it, as it will become a distraction.

Precautions

Any scientific programming requires proper guidance and precautions that should be followed and Neuro Linguistic Program is no different. However, it must be noted that NLP has no side effects but this does not mean care and caution should not be exercised. The main issue that happens when not exercising caution is that the effects of NLP may not come. This could also imply that you may see delayed results or that the tasks will not be carried out as planned.

• The main ideology behind NLP is comparison and hence the main thing to remember is that you don't make extensive comparisons. Extract comparisons and find main differences from situations and people. Make pointers of these in a positive manner and use them. Keep a realistic approach. Don't overestimating or underestimate. Overestimating a person's ability and shrinking your abilities in comparison to them will not give you the desired effects. Overestimating yourself and undermining people will also have a negative effect. Accept your flaws, negative points and do the same with people and situations. Keep yourself open to questioning yourself and improving yourself through self-analysis.

• Neuro Linguistic Program is used to bring clarity, precision and focus through organization of your thoughts. It helps to control actions and emotions and takes a very nonjudgmental outlook. However, that does not imply being robotic. Emotions are not a bad thing and they are what make us inherently human. Don't shun your emotions away. Emotions like passion, desire, hope are those that help you achieve your goal. These are also what make personal connections with people. Overusing your emotions is also wrong as it makes you very volatile. This can hinder success and at the same time making yourself completely devoid of emotions makes you cold and aloof. This can make people perceive you to be insensitive or frigid. This can rub people the wrong way.

• It is imperative to stay focused and concentrate on the task at hand. It is this focus and devotion that brings you success. Now it is important to be flexible. Goals will alter as situations and circumstances change but ensure that you are more flexible with the method and course of action rather than just the goal as this would lead to confusion. When setting a goal try to estimate yourself and the course of action you need to take. Take your time and be patient with yourself when setting a goal. Focus on the goal and make it practical and feasible. Modify your goals only when need be. Don't change and alter the program unless required to. This is a scientific program and thus makes use of analysis and evaluation. This gives little room for flexibility and alternation. Abide by the rules and analyze facts as they are.

• Make proper estimations of yourself. Have reasonable expectations and don't expect too high or aim too low. NLP is a scientific program that impacts people differently. It works on the basis of your abilities. If someone obtains the effects of NLP in a few months, it does not imply that you too will get your results within a few months. The time period for every person varies. This is because all of us are trained in a different way. Our minds work differently and we are tuned to different aspects. Also having a lot of high expectation can often lead to disappointments when it is not met. This will reduce your focus and clarity. Be in control of yourself and make realistic assumptions of yourself. There are several ways through which you can be trained, choose one that is best suited for you and remember that training takes time.

Applications

It must be noted that NLP can be applied at any point in life and in any field as well. It can be used in relationships, in your social life, in your professional life and so on. The basic principles behind NLP remains the same and the only small differences lie in the field in which you want to implement it. In this chapter we will take a look at how NLP is applied in various fields.

Relationships:

Relationships are some areas most people fail at, this is because they are abstract and are very hard to manage. This also attributes to our stressful lives; lack of time and lack of clarity in our communication and this makes people lose patience with us. There are various cases where this can lead to breakups, estranged relationships and separated couples. Conversations end up becoming arguments and in several cases there are times when even family members don't talk to each other. This leads to alienation.

With NLP, fostering better relationships is possible. It increases discipline and makes us reduce conflicts in our personal life. We are more conscious and aware of what we speak and do through NLP. We evaluate and take control of the situation. It is in these cases that even when an argument breaks out, we are conscious enough to avoid it or move our way around it. The unconscious mind also prevents our conscious mind from acting aggressively. This is because in NLP, the unconscious parts of the mind are also triggered. These parts are deep rooted into your minds and control them involuntarily. Thus, the subconscious and the unconscious parts of the mind are sharper and perceptive.

In a certain way, since we start to sort out our thoughts and perspective, NLP helps us to speak only matters of importance. People who undergo NLP training are more patient, more understanding and are more sensitive towards people. This increases compatibility and enhances compromise. This will in turn make the relationship work. Conflict of ideas and opinions are something that is

common and NLP recognizes this and allows negative
emotions building up.

If there are conflicts because of varied views on a certain
matter, the NLP trained mind helps to reach a middle
ground without conflicts. Even if this is not possible due to
the complete opposition of views, NLP aims at making the
person more sensitive and they are able to respect the
other person's views. It reduces argumentative nature by
reducing aggressive nature and tendencies to fight. This
will save a lot of botheration.

NLP also reduces problematic relationships. In today's era,
long distance relationships are a common phenomenon.
With people living in different parts of the world and
placing equal importance to career, it can lead to distrust
and infidelity when focus shifts. With distance and time
differences people often forget their previous relationships
and move on with life. NLP aims at making people more
focused towards themselves. It increases our morale and
confidence by reducing our distraction so that we remain
faithful and not succumb to cheating and other lowly
aspects. It makes us more conscious and we stop making
decisions based on our sole emotions.

Creative jobs:

NLP makes us more creative and this is very important in
creative jobs. It removes misconceptions, preformed
notions and makes the mind more open. We become more
flexible and adjusting towards things and this facilitates
people in creative fields like painting, acting, writing etc.
The mind also channels creativity effectively and makes it
more risk taking. The principles of the risk reward theory

work here. It also makes us more inspired by making our minds more conscious. When we exercise our minds completely, we are able to develop new thoughts and ideas. These ideas can be implemented well through analysis and evaluation. Thus it creates a harmony between our analytical parts of the brain and the creative side of it.

High Stress Jobs:

High stress jobs include jobs where professional are always on their toes. Some examples of such jobs are jobs in like medical fields, legal fields, security etc. It deals with people and there can be several emergency cases that lead to odd timings. When all this takes place it is very easy to get stressed out and start panicking. NLP aims at rescuing this and maintain a peace of mind. Loss of focus can cost the person their jobs and therefore maintain focus and accuracy is key. These jobs are very frustrating and may hamper the patience of the person and the mind becomes attuned to the high levels of stress. Even when the person is resting, the mind is constantly active increasing brain clutter. People who have been trained in NLP deal with the stress a lot more efficiently. They are able to find a bridge between personal and professional lives. They are able to make better decisions with greater accuracy. It also reduces the amount of mental breakdowns people end up having. People are more in control of themselves.

Planning Jobs:

Marketing jobs in business, event management, engineering and other such jobs require lots of planning. This is one of the benefits of NLP training. It helps us plan better. It makes us focused and helps in goal achievement by working towards the target. This is done through planning; it helps us plan better by decluttering our mind. It helps us to sort our thoughts and think ahead. It also benefits the parts of the brain that are used for decision making. It evaluates analyses and declutters thoughts to make it comprehensible. Even in projects that require quick decision-making, NLP serves to be very useful. It facilitates efficiency and increases the speed at which we work.

Social Life:

In today's era social life plays a pivotal role in shaping our views and personalities. While relationships are also very important, the emphasis placed on social life cannot be denied. Meeting new people and establishing contacts are often the driving forces of goal achievement in today's context. Meeting new people increases our exposure towards new experiences and visiting uncharted territories. It also broadens ours perspective and makes us more knowledgeable. This is turn will boost our self-esteem and increases the ability with which we handle people. While some people have a large social circle, others don't and this is not a bad thing. The important aspect is handling people in any circle be it small or large. The social life that we lead should also be a reflection of what we believe in and we should be able to manage this. This implies that we should not get distracted and wavered by it. We should also not make it interfere in our personal lives.

Having a messy social life can lead to problems. This will reduce your interpersonal skills and make your communication unclear. This is where NLP becomes useful. NLP aims at reducing distractions and thus increases our communication by letting us segregate what we are thinking and putting that into words in a precise manner. It makes us more empathetic as we stop voicing out our opinions that would belittle others. We make conscious efforts to be more effective in what we do. We also find a balance between confidence and humbleness. NLP helps in achieving this balance by training our minds. NLP imbibes in us qualities like open mindedness to increase our exposure. We reduce stereotyping and generalizing. This in turn will give us a healthy environment to work with.

NLP and Hypnosis

NLP is often used in combination with hypnosis. This is done to make the training and process a lot more efficient. The main aim of hypnosis is to achieve maximum concentration. The objective is to remove any distraction and hindrances; this would make the person's mind free for control and manipulation. NLP can often be seen as an abstract art that could take time to develop, to increase the retention of the mind, hypnosis is used. The combination of the two helps to instruct the mind.

Our mind gets focused on a particular detail or thought when we are hypnotized. The hypnotizer or the trainers aims to reduce distractions and noise until our focus is on one thing. We concentrate on a particular point and this makes our senses more receptive. It also makes the mind more active and open by being receptive to receiving more signals. When this takes place, NLP training is incorporated. Points are stated and emphasized on so that it stays in our mind. Since we will not be distracted and our mind remains relatively empty, it is easier for the mind to accept this information and store it for a long time. Also, in this state the mind will perceive all instructions as facts instead of goals, thus the mind directs us to perform certain tasks a lot better. There are various other methods that are utilized depending on the subject. NLP can also be performed without a trainer through self-hypnosis. Listed below are a few ways through which you can hypnotize yourself for the purpose of NLP.

• Start by becoming comfortable. Wear comfortable clothes and reduce all constrictive articles of clothing like watches, belts, sashes, etc. Wear loose fitting clothes that help you breathe evenly made of light weight materials.

• Similarly ensure that you are in a comfortable environment. Let the room be clean, smell fresh and make you feel comfortable. Reduce all distraction and clutter in the room. Switch off the TV, switch off your phone and stay away from gadgets for a good 30 to 45 minutes. Ensure that the temperature of the room is also according to your requirement. The room shouldn't be too hot nor should it be too cold.

• Sit in a comfortable chair in a position that suits you and shut the door or ask people to not disturb you for a while.

• Once you have sat in a comfortable position, start by thinking of your goals and your objectives. Speak in a clear voice to yourself and state this in present tense. Also, ensure that you speak like it is already happening. For instance, instead of saying, "I want to quit smoking", say, "I have quit smoking and I feel a lot better about it."

• Relax your mind and body. Maintain a good posture and avoid crossing your arms and legs because you will start to fidget out of discomfort soon. Focus on part of the body at a time and try to relax it. Relax each part little by little and think of a comforting place or surrounding like a garden or a valley. This will calm your senses faster. Use extensive imagery that is comforting and soothing. If you don't feel completely relaxed, don't panic. This will increase distraction. Let thoughts flow into your mind and keep trying to get relaxed.

• Once you feel that your body is properly relaxed, start by breathing in and out at a good slow pace. Ensure that you are aware of your breathing. Breathe in like you are inhaling a good pleasing scent and exhale imaging that you are releasing all the toxic from your lungs. This action of inhalation and exhalation is therapeutic and lets you calm down. Keep doing this process until you feel like you are floating. When you have attained this stage, you have entered the hypnotic trance.

• When this happens, keep reciting your goals. Use positive words and words of encouragement. Avoid any negative terms. For instance, instead of saying, "I don't want to fail", state "I will succeed with great results". Negative words get stored in the unconscious parts of the mind and this can impact your actions. Also, it is very hard to alter the unconscious mind. Also envision your thoughts, envision your actions and imagine that what you are saying is truly happening. You will immediately be able to see yourself in that situation and you will feel happy.

•   After a few moments of doing this, start by erasing your imagination. Stop envisioning and imagining and start thinking instead. Start this process slowly; imagine that you are in your present situation. The chair you are sitting in, the room that you are in and the clothes you are wearing. Keep increasing this in real time until you feel that you have completely come out of your imagination. Once this is done, open your eyes slowly and breathe in and out slowly and steadily as you open them.

•   You can repeat this process twice to thrice a day and you can do this for a period of 30 minutes. This will maximize the results and increase your ability to achieve your goals.

Frequently Asked Questions

Is NLP a form of science and is it a scientific program?

Yes, NLP actually is a scientific method and derives its principles from neurology. It is through these principles and the scientific study of the brain that helps to produce ideal results. It is often considered a form of pseudoscience. This is attributed because of the lack of knowledge with regards to the functioning of the central nervous system. It is also abstract as it trains the mind through disciple and organization. It helps to clarify thoughts and segregate information in a systematic manner to help recall memories and increase the precision and accuracy of the brain. Observation is one of the primary tools that are used in NLP. Facts are observed and evaluated. These are weighed in terms of importance and those that are not required are often discarded. NLP is an art form that trains the mind and treats it much like a computer just like how any scientific program works.

What is the significance of NLP?

NLP is often mistaken to be another form of self-improvement program. However, this is not true. NLP provides long-term effects and benefits to the mind. The main aim of NLP is that it provides clarity and focus. It focuses the thoughts and information by segregating them and storing them even in the unconscious parts of the mind that are often inaccessible. This increases the impact of the information aiding memory. NLP lets us tap our hidden talents and explore possibilities. It keeps us in self-control and makes the mind more accurate. It helps control negative aspects create a sound environment, reduce addictions and so on. For instance, it can reduce negative emotions and feelings such as hate, anger, misery, jealousy and so on. This can increase the personal aspects of yourself and enhance your interpersonal skills. It is also beneficial in the professional realm by drawing attention of issues, providing quick solutions, focus, precision and quicker response. In fact, NLP offers all around development.

Is there an Age Limit for Practicing NLP?

No, there isn't any particular age that is required to practice this art form. It can be taken up by anyone at any stage. It is beneficial to everybody including young people, teenagers, old people and so on. It has a holistic approach and does not clutter the brain through memorization and information overload. It is more of a practical know how that makes us reflect on the kind of abilities we want. NLP has also gained popularity in modern times to treat memory related problems in older people. It is used in psychiatry and psychology to control the mind. It also reduces the onset of attention deficit disorders and reduces the distraction of children and keeps them more focused.

Is the training long lasting or is it possible to forget aspects that are discussed during training?

No, the best thing about NLP is that any training and development that you receive will be stuck with you. NLP makes use of the complete mind and channels information even to the dormant parts of the mind like the unconscious parts. The information from the training moves between the conscious mind, subconscious and the unconscious mind thus increasing the impact of the information. These traits end up becoming our commands and thus are reproduced in our personalities. However, altering thoughts is possible with NLP, if anyone wants to change something that they learned in the NLP training then in order to reverse it a different NLP approach must be used. The main point to note is that your mind should have valid sizable reasons on why that particular information is rejected only then will the rest of the mind comply, else it will reject the discarding process.

Does getting trained in NLP involve lots of study and hard work?

No, NLP is not a study nor is it something that will be tested. It isn't an intellectual process but rather a method to alter behavioral conditions that arises out of information in our unconscious and subconscious minds. There are specialized training done for NLP and the success rate depends on your abilities. It however does require some amount of practice.

Conclusion

Hypnosis is an extremely powerful tool that can be beneficial or detrimental, depending on how it is used. Only people with pure intentions should use the art of hypnotizing people because there are moral obligations that should be upheld during all portions of the process.

Remember, it is rude to pick around in someone's subconscious for the joy of doing so. You should ensure that you are mentally prepared to handle anything that may come your way. If you notice that the person you are hypnotizing is experiencing any type of distress, you should stop immediately and return them to a full state of consciousness.

The Dangers of Hypnotizing

There are many dangers that you can run into if you try to hypnotize someone without proper training. The truth is, when someone is hypnotized, you are playing with a vulnerable subconscious and without proper training, and you can easily cause permanent damage to their psyche. It is important that you become properly trained and that you truly understand the basics of psychology before you enter the world of hypnotism.

Understanding how the human mind works at its most vulnerable states can help you prevent harming someone long term or causing them to develop fears and phobias that did not previously exist.

The most important thing to remember when diving into someone subconscious is that you have the power to open up memories that they are not ready to face yet. This can cause severe emotional trauma to those who are already "mentally vulnerable."

It is wise to screen the people you hypnotize carefully to ensure that they have not endured any childhood trauma. This is because under hypnosis, these memories can become extremely vivid and the subject may not be able to handle the pain associated with the memories you are unknowingly digging up.

Screen Your Research

There are thousands, if not millions of websites that focus on hypnosis. Of these websites, the majority of them do not give proper advice to the novice hypnotists. Following advice blindly can result in failing to hypnotize the person, or can cause serious harm to your subject. Learn what websites and books are written by reputable sources and ensure that you follow the directions completely. Just because you become more experienced in hypnotizing does not mean that you can skip steps or take less precautions when hypnotizing people.

Make sure that you only follow the advice of professionals, seek professional advice if you are unsure about the information that you have obtained online.

Take Classes

There are many locations that offer classes on hypnotizing. This is the safest route to go if you want to ensure the mental stability of your subjects before, and after they are hypnotized. It is also a great resource if you are looking for advice on getting a waiver in place for you subjects, just in case they do not divulge all of the information you request in your screening process.

Bonus

Thanks for making it this far in your education. If you want the real multiplier effect and to take your hypnosis skills to the next level, I recommend the easy-to-follow quick tips below to help you unlock more time so you can focus on learning and applying the techniques you care about (e.g. mind control, hypnosis, etc.). No matter what your interests are in life, everyone can benefit from ways to be more productive and time efficient. Minimize time and energy spent on things you don't care about, so you can maximize on what you do!

Visit https://funnelb.leadpages.co/smarter-not-harder-business/

Top 10 Productivity Tips & Hacks GUARANTEED to Unlock Massive Amounts of Time, Crush Decision Fatigue, and Skyrocket Your Efficiency and Effectiveness

EXACT BLUEPRINT on How to Hypnotize Anyone, Including Yourself - Mind Control, Self-Hypnosis, and NLP

Link: https://funnelb.leadpages.co/smarter-not-harder-business/

www.ingramcontent.com/pod-product-compliance
Lightning Source LLC
Chambersburg PA
CBHW070419290526
45791CB00005B/1760